# Developing Restorative Connections

## A Workbook for Lay Counselors and Community Builders

Susan Oh Cha, Ph.D.

LifeNote Press

Author photograph by Mindy Webb
Cover and interior design by Daria Lacy

ISBN 978-0-9836551-2-1

Printed in the United States of America

The Spirit of the Sovereign Lord is on me,
because the Lord has anointed me
to proclaim good news to the poor.
He has sent me to bind up the brokenhearted,
to proclaim freedom for the captives and
release from darkness for the prisoners,
to proclaim the year of the Lord's favor and
the day of vengeance of our God,
to comfort all who mourn,
and provide for those who grieve in Zion—
to bestow on them a crown of beauty  instead of ashes,
the oil of joy instead of mourning, and
a garment of praise instead of a spirit of despair.
They will be called oaks of righteousness,
a planting of the Lord for the display of his splendor.
Isaiah 61:1-3 (NIV)

# Contents

# Introduction

When I was growing up in the church, God moved my heart and mind to recognize how individuals, couples, and families were suffering and to work toward engendering emotional healing and health in these people whom God loved. By allowing God to work through us to bring restoration in and between people, the church can become healthier and better able to function as a truer reflection of God. This hope is at the core of this workbook.

I am excited to share this training curriculum with you. It is structured to provide information, time for reflection, and opportunity to practice counseling tools in order to facilitate your own healing as well as encourage others' well-being. Open and honest sharing of your personal thoughts and feelings is recommended as this will help with learning and growth in your lay counseling ministry. In order to promote candid discussions, it is essential to keep all information in sessions confidential.

It is my prayer that God will use you to "bind up the brokenhearted," "proclaim freedom...from darkness," "comfort all who mourn," and "bestow... beauty...joy" into the lives of people you are privileged to counsel (Isaiah 61:1-3 NIV).

# Session 1

## Model for Lay Counseling Ministry in the Church

One of my favorite stories in the Bible depicts Jesus being confronted by the Jewish leaders regarding a woman's adulterous behavior.[1] They bring her to him, not because of any real desire to do what is right, but to entrap Jesus. Their ploy does not work. Instead, they are confronted with their own sins and are compelled to leave her alone. Unlike the men who humiliated and degraded this woman, Jesus extends mercy and grace towards her. He does not condemn her; however, he directs her to begin a new life. He balances beautifully love and justice in this interchange. I believe what Jesus manifests here is a model for healthy counseling: approaching someone who is hurting with compassion while simultaneously addressing the wrong choices the person has made with biblical truths and empowering that individual to begin anew.

*There are three main characters (religious leaders, adulterous woman, and Jesus) depicted in the above story: Which one do you identify with the most and why?*

_____

_____

_____

_____

## Being Part of the Whole

We are part of the "body of Christ," the church. What is a "church"? This word originates from the Greek word, *ekklesia*, meaning, "call out" and "assembly." Thus, church is an assembly of believers called out by Jesus to love God and one another. We have been joined together to have "equal concern for each other. If one part suffers, every part suffers with it; if one part is honored, every part rejoices with it."[2] Our choices impact our community, sometimes in obvious ways, and many times, in subtle and even invisible ways. If a part of our body is injured, the whole body suffers. Even a toothache has the power to make us lose concentration, feel tired and irritable, and reduce motivation to do anything. If a church member is depressed, this affects her family – both biological and spiritual. And how we respond to her pain makes a difference not only to her health but also to the health of the greater family that is the church.

It is important to "carry each other's burdens" and "carry [our] own load" as Paul urges in his letter to the people in Galatia.[3] At first glance this may seem like a contradiction, but Paul uses two different Greek words in Galatians 6:2 and 6:5 – one signifies a "burden" too heavy to carry unassisted, while the other represents a lighter "load" that one can bear alone. These two verses depict a healthy integration of how we are to function within the family of Christ. We are called to love and serve others, especially those who are more vulnerable and/or unable to care for themselves. We are also called to take responsibility for our own lives – whether it is in the using of our talents, holding ourselves accountable for our choices, and/or doing the best we can with what we are given. By caring for others, we are also caring for ourselves, because what others do affects our well-being (and vice versa) as we are part of the same family. In essence, loving others and loving ourselves are two sides of the same coin.

*Write an example of how you love others as well as yourself:*

_____

_____

_____

## Importance of Lay Counseling

Some people in the church are not well equipped to love themselves or others in healthy ways. They may suffer from mental health issues, which interfere with their ability to function well – spiritually, relationally, and emotionally. They affect the church as a whole: The more parts of our body that are injured, the weaker and unhealthier we become. This then impacts the work we can do for Christ in our neighborhoods and the global community.

Just as we seek medical help for physical problems, we need to seek psychological help for mental disorders. However, many people in the church are reluctant to invite mental health professionals into their lives due to feelings of shame (e.g., "I can't let anyone see what's really going on"), fear (e.g., "What if they think I'm crazy?"), denial (e.g., "Others live like this too. My situation isn't that bad") and/or resignation to life as is (e.g., "There's nothing more I can do"). It is understandable that individuals and families are resistant to beginning psychological treatments, especially when they have limited understanding of what these entail. For ethnic minority communities, there is an added issue of having only a limited number of bilingual Christian psychotherapists. What this means is that (a) one does not have much choice in whom one sees; (b) the possibility of multiple roles increases, which may contaminate the therapeutic relationship or process; and (c) one might need to wait a long time for an opening in the professional's schedule before being able to get the help he needs. Another factor that interferes with people seeking professional treatment involves cost: Psychotherapy requires significant financial investment, which many cannot afford.

For these church members, it is helpful to have a network of trained lay (i.e., nonprofessional) counselors in the church who can provide prayer, support, encouragement, and guidance to help them heal and change in positive ways. These trained counselors can also work alongside the pastoral staff to meet with those who are suffering due to individual, marital, and/or family issues, thereby sharing the burden of caring for them. We can also strengthen each member of the church and the church itself by offering support groups that these trained counselors would facilitate: groups for single parents, people who suffer from depression, those recovering from addictions, parents struggling with children who have special needs, etc.

*List any areas that you feel particularly passionate about within the mental health realm:*

_____

_____

_____

_____

**Practical Considerations for Lay Counselors**

In order to work with diverse types of people and issues that may surface, it is important to select lay counselors who have a deep, abiding faith in God, passion for helping others heal and grow, and talent for counseling. The latter includes spiritual gifts of knowledge, wisdom, discernment, and encouragement as well as personal characteristics of warmth, compassion, and genuine interest in people. It is also helpful to have counselors who have experienced some form of emotional and relational distress that they have adaptively worked through. Other helpful traits include: patience, openness, being able to listen well, and ability to keep information confidential.

As a prospective lay counselor, if you are not sure whether your talents lean in this direction, this 12-session training will hopefully bring clarity and conviction. These sessions will cover various topics, such as, communication, counseling tools, common mental disorders, legal and ethical issues, and when and how to refer clients who are beyond the scope of what lay counselors can do. Lay counselors need to be supervised by pastors and/or mental health professionals on a regular basis, either in group or individual formats.

After the 12-session training, those who are called to serve as lay counselors may be ready to be matched with congregation members who ask for counseling. They may be contacted through the church leaders who are overseeing this ministry. It is important to have an initial meeting to see if the lay counselor and the client are a good fit, e.g., do both parties feel comfortable with one another? If they decide that they are not well suited to work together, they can approach the lay counseling ministry leaders to find a different match. If they decide to proceed with the counseling, they can choose the time and place that is convenient for them. All meetings should be 30 minutes to 90 minutes in length depending on what is being discussed and how much help is needed.

*As you begin to consider how well this ministry fits you, reflect on your spiritual gifts, personality, communication style, and life experiences:*

_____

_____

_____

_____

_____

_____

_____

## Fundamental Principles of Lay Counseling

The following are principles of effective lay counseling ministry:

- Invite God to be the center of your ministry. Pray for the work you are doing as well as for the person you are counseling. Use the Bible as a fundamental guide. This does not mean that you quote Scripture at every meeting, but that your work is consistent with what is written in the Bible.

- Continually pursue spiritual, emotional, and relational health for yourself even as you help others toward this goal. For example, spend time with God; engage in self-reflection and growth; and be actively involved with family, friends, and volunteer organizations.

- Be respectful of your client. She may have made wrong choices, behave in ways that are hurtful to others, and/or be someone you are not naturally inclined to like. Nonetheless, God loves her, and God has placed her in your life for a purpose. It is up to you and your client to explore and understand what this is, and also to work together to change those aspects of her life that are interfering with God's will for her.

Ultimately, I pray that we can say of our ministry: work that is produced by faith, labor that is prompted by love, and endurance that is inspired by hope in our Lord Jesus Christ.[4]

# Session 2

## Building the Relational Context

I have always been impressed by how Jesus connects with all types of people: religious leaders, teachers of the law, fishermen, children, various racial groups, disciples, as well as those who are spiritually, mentally, and physically disabled. He relates to them from a place of knowing himself and realizing his purpose.[1] Thus, he is not influenced by public opinions nor by a desire to please people, but rather, He is focused on being and doing what He is called to do.[2] Jesus starts from here to engage people in authentic, straightforward, and personal ways across many situations, and in others, by using parables to communicate his thoughts and feelings.

One of the most familiar biblical stories is the *Parable of the Good Samaritan*.[3] There are many wonderful messages in this parable. For our purposes, I would like to center on how Jesus connects with the Jewish lawyer who prompts Jesus to narrate this story. When the latter approaches Jesus with questions, it would have been much easier for Jesus to just answer his questions directly. Instead, He invites the lawyer to reflect and examine his heart and mind for the answers by asking questions and using an allegory. In doing this, Jesus engenders further knowledge and understanding in the lawyer. As counselors, it is important (a) to connect to different types of people God brings to you; (b) to be grounded in God and His purpose for you and your ministry; and (c) to relate to people in ways that empower them.

*What kinds of people do you have more trouble befriending and/or being a "neighbor" to?*

_____

_____

_____

_____

## Establishing Rapport

More than any techniques or tools, what makes counseling effective is the affinity between the counselor and the client. From the first contact, everything is noted and categorized, consciously and unconsciously. How you speak, where you meet, whether you are prompt, how you are dressed, what you say or do not say, who your family members and friends are, etc., all contribute to a lasting impression that can establish or destroy rapport. Thus, it is important to be aware of how you appear to others, acknowledge it, and modify your behaviors where necessary, to build your relationship with your client.

*What are some assumptions people might make about you based on how you present yourself?*

_____

_____

_____

_____

A therapeutic relationship is founded on authenticity, connectedness, and purpose. Being authentic means that you are honest and genuine in your approach, and confident in who you are and what you believe in, so that you do not become codependent with your client. It is essential not to be motivated by wanting to please and wanting your client to like you. This will interfere with working effectively with your client. Instead, be clear about your own thoughts and feelings about various issues and how you can use these to help your client have more insight into his own situation.

It is also imperative to be empathetic, warm, and engaging with your client so that she feels cared for, understood, and accepted. In order to help your client, you must understand the situation from her perspective, and then be able to articulate what you heard. By sharing your understanding, you give her the opportunity to correct any misconceptions; you let the person know you have been listening closely, which will encourage further elaboration; and you help her gain clarity into her own thoughts and feelings.

The following are some behaviors that are not conducive to a positive working relationship: preaching at your client, arguing with your client, talking too much about yourself and how you have been successful in the areas the person is struggling with, not paying attention to what your client is sharing, thinking about what you have to do after the meeting, talking about your own issues, and falling asleep (believe it or not, this has been reported to occur). These behaviors will not only cause a disconnect which will negatively impact the developing relationship but also harm the client's sense of self, trust, and hope.

Establishing rapport also necessitates having a clear purpose for your meetings. By the time someone asks for counseling, he is most likely feeling stressed, confused, helpless, and lost. It is important to offer him a sense of direction and hope by identifying and clarifying the issues as well as exploring possibilities for change. Your client needs to come away from these meetings feeling more encouraged and motivated to help himself.

*What do you think will be your pitfalls in establishing rapport with your clients?*

_____

_____

_____

## Asking Questions

One of the primary ways to build relationships is to ask questions. Asking questions can lead to beginnings of a relationship and/or can sustain one. It can create feelings of care and concern. When we follow-up on a person's comment with further questions, we are demonstrating attentiveness and interest. It is important to ask questions in a way that makes your client feel comfortable and gives her an opportunity to be open and willing to express her thoughts and feelings. Try to ask open-ended questions that can lead to descriptive answers rather than monosyllabic responses.

Do not use questions to criticize and demean your client: For example, "How could you do that?!" Do not ask questions to showcase how knowledgeable you are: For example, your client wonders whether he should get a divorce, and you say, "You know what the Bible says about divorce, right? What does Jesus say in Matthew 19:3-9?" Do not use questions as a diving board to talk about yourself: For example, you ask, "Do you play any music?" so that you can share how you play multiple musical instruments. Instead, your questions should help your client learn about himself, his vulnerabilities, and his journey, so that, he does the work of figuring out what he needs and how to get there.

*The following are some examples of questions you can ask. Please re-word them to increase their effectiveness:*

Why are you here?

_____

Who do you get along with at home?

_____

Do you feel good about that decision?

_____

Do you want to look at what God says about that?

_____

How did you let your relationship get so bad?

_____

Why didn't you seek help sooner?

_____

## Listening Reflectively

Reflective listening is the most fundamental skill needed for counseling. It refers to an active, nonjudgmental, focused listening, which involves grasping what the other thinks and feels, and then stating what you heard so that the other feels understood and validated. It also involves attending to nonverbal cues, such as, eye contact, speech patterns, tone, gestures, and body language, and reflecting what you observe. You are, in essence, providing a mirror for the other to see herself more clearly and to consider a problem more rationally.

When you reflect back what you hear and see, it is important to keep your statements tentative. None of us can be positive that we know exactly what the other is feeling, thus, it is critical to watch our tone and words so that we do not come across like a mind reader. Use discretion and sensitivity in recognizing what is best to reflect. When you are responding to what you hear and see, begin by asking yourself, "What is he feeling?" and respond to his feelings. Here is a template of how to construct a reflective listening response: "It sounds like you feel _____ because_____."

_Practice reflective listening:_

Speaker: "I'm so upset that this friend never follows through on her commitments."

Reflective Listening Response:

_____

Speaker: "I can never do anything right. So what's the point of
  trying?"

Reflective Listening Response:

_____

Speaker: "I did what you said, but it didn't help."

Reflective Listening Response:

_____

Speaker: "I thought I was going to get a promotion, but I didn't."

Reflective Listening Response:

_____

Speaker: "I think my husband is having an affair. I don't know
  what to do."

Reflective Listening Response:

_____

Speaker: "I don't know what's going on with my older daughter.
  She's really changed."

Reflective Listening Response:

_____

**Exploring Alternatives**

Through asking questions and listening reflectively, you and your client will have a better understanding of the difficulties the latter is facing. Sometimes, just the experience of being heard might be sufficient for your client to discover solutions to his problems on his own. There are other times when he might need further help in determining the best course of action. As lay counselors, you can find resolutions for his concerns by exploring options together and encouraging him to make a decision that makes the most sense to him (which may not be the one you might choose).

The process of exploring alternatives should not be confused with giving advice. Giving advice, such as, "Why don't you do this..." or "I think you should..." is generally not helpful in a counseling relationship. Advice does not help your client learn to solve her own problems. It can deprive her of a great opportunity to learn and grow from her own decisions. It encourages her to be dependent upon you. This may make you feel good as you are looked upon as "the expert," but it can leave her feeling "less than," insecure, and inadequate. In addition, many people resist taking advice. They are either skeptical that your advice will work, or they do not want to do what you are suggesting, or there are underlying issues that cause them to unconsciously fight against it. This then negatively affects your counseling relationship. Furthermore, if your advice does not lead to a desirable outcome, you are held responsible: You are blamed. If it works, you get the credit and become disproportionately important in their lives. This is not a healthy place to be. It is better to empower your clients to take responsibility for their own choices.

Instead of giving advice, practice exploring alternatives together. Steps in considering possible options include:

- Summarizing the presenting problem(s). This includes recognizing:

  - Precipitating contributors to the issues

  - Duration and magnitude of the troubles

  - Efforts that have been made to resolve the problems

- Brainstorming

  - "Shall we look at some choices you have about this?"

- Assisting your client to choose a solution by evaluating the various possibilities

  - "Which idea do you think would work best for you?"

- Discussing the probable results of the decision

  - "What do you think will happen if you do that?"

- Obtaining a commitment to action

  - "What have you decided to do?"

- Planning a time for evaluation

  - "When shall we discuss this again?"

Be careful to not enter into exploring alternatives too soon. If you move too fast, your client may not be ready, and thus, refuse to participate in the above process in obvious and subtle ways.

*Here is a sample script depicting how you might explore alternatives with your client:*

Client: "I hate school. I don't want to go to school."

Counselor: (Having asked questions and listened reflectively prior to the above statement, you can now summarize the issue) "I understand that ever since your teacher made fun of you in class about a week ago, you have not wanted to go to school. It's gotten so bad this week that you weren't able to go to school today even though you tried to make yourself go."

Client: "Yeah...I just can't go to school anymore."

Counselor: "Is there anything you, your parents, and/or I can do to help you with this?"

Client: "Convince my parents to not force me to go to school... or I can move to a different school... or I can be home-schooled."

Counselor: "It's great that you are able to come up with these options. Where shall we start first?"

Client: "Maybe home-schooling."

Counselor: "What do you think will happen if you do that?"

Client: "I think it will be better."

Counselor: "This will mean that your mom/dad will be home with you a lot: teaching and grading your work. How would that be for you?"

Client: "That would suck. I don't want that."

Counselor: "What would you like to try instead?"

Client: "Maybe if my parents paid me to go to school..."

Counselor: "That's another idea. What do you think will happen if you ask your parents for money to go to school?"

Client: "They'll probably not give it to me. Or give me so little that it won't make a difference."

Counselor: "So it sounds like that won't work either? You have mentioned lots of options thus far – not going to school altogether, moving to a different school, home-schooling, getting money to go to school – which one do you think will help you the most to work through this?"

Client: "Actually, I think the best thing for me to do is to talk to my teacher."

Counselor: "What do you think will happen if you do that?"

Client: "Although it will be really hard to go up to him, I can maybe have a better understanding of where the teacher was coming from... maybe I just misunderstood...maybe he's just a jerk in which case I can have my parents talk with him."

Counselor: "So, this is what you will do then?"

Client: "Yeah."

Counselor: "When will you talk with your teacher?"

Client: "Tomorrow."

Counselor: "Let me know how it goes. Can we talk after school at 4pm?"

Client: "OK."

*What do you see as your areas for growth as you try to explore alternatives with your client?*

_____

_____

_____

_____

*The following are scenarios to practice what you learned from this session with a partner:*

Client: "I am feeling overwhelmed and can't get things done."

Client: "My daughter is spending all of her extra-curricular time with her friends who are bad influences."

Client: "My parents fight all the time."

Client: "I'm so sick of picking up after my husband and the kids. Why can't they be responsible for taking care of their own stuff?"

Client: "My spouse never seems to have time for me."

Client: "My parents constantly yell at me about grades."

Client: "No one likes me."

Client: "God never answers my prayers."

Client: "My son always forgets what his assignments are, and not only that, forgets to turn in his assignments."

Client: "My parents expect too much from me. I'm so tired of trying to meet their expectations."

Client: "I think my teenager is addicted to computer games."

Client: "My wife is always critical. Everything is an issue with her."

Client: "Saying yes is not the problem in my house. Follow-through is."

Client: "How do I know if my teenager is using marijuana?"

Client: "When my spouse gets angry, he stays that way for a long time."

*What is the most difficult aspect of the above practice?*

_____

_____

_____

_____

Many of you will find that you are better at one approach than another. As you continue to practice *establishing rapport, asking questions, listening reflectively,* and *exploring alternatives,* you will find that these skills become more natural and easier to apply in your lay counseling work. Using these ways of connecting with people facilitates healthy relationships in your personal lives as well. Even as you work to help your "neighbor," you are also helping yourself.

# Session 3

## Counseling Tools

What is Jesus' underlying tool when engaging with the world and the people in it? Prayer. He spent time praying alone to stay connected to God and to prepare Himself for His ministry.[1] He spent time praying with and for people.[2] And ultimately, he prayed for God's will to be done through Him.[3]

This then is the first tool for lay counselors. It is essential to be connected to God through prayer as you serve in this ministry. Even as you work hard to master the concepts and techniques in this curriculum, ask God to give you the wisdom, knowledge, and love to minister to His people effectively. Also, if your clients ask for prayer during your meetings, feel free to pray with them. If, on the other hand, they do not want this, do not try to persuade them to pray with you. Instead, accept them where they are, and use other tools. Lastly, it is helpful to pray for your clients, especially before and after your meetings, as this centers you and your work in Christ, making you a more powerful lay counselor.

In addition to prayer, there are many other techniques that are effective for promoting health. We will focus on those that are easier to learn and implement: deep breathing, biblical meditation, guided imagery, journaling, cognitive restructuring, role-playing, and using media.

## Deep Breathing

Breathing in short, shallow bursts engages the sympathetic nervous system, which is activated by stress and is correlated with various disorders. Deep breathing, on the other hand, engages the para-sympathetic nervous system, which is activated when we are calm and relaxed. Deep breathing is beneficial to our mind and body. It has been empirically studied to demonstrate positive effects on our heart, brain, immune system, and mental health.[4] It releases endorphins in our brains. This can lead to decrease in pain. It can improve concentration and focus. When you are taking deep breaths, it sends signals to your brain that you are at peace, and your brain, in turn, sends signals to your body confirming that all is well.

*Practice deep breathing by yourself and with your clients:*

- Lie down on the floor. Bend your knees and move your feet about shoulder length apart. Place one hand on your abdomen and one hand on your chest.

- Inhale slowly and deeply through your nose into your abdomen to push up your hand as much as you feel comfortable. Your chest should move only a little and only with your abdomen. Inhale for a count of three-five seconds.

- Hold your breath for a count of five seconds.

- Exhale through your mouth, almost as if you are blowing out a candle. Do this for a count of five-eight seconds. Your abdomen should contract as you exhale.

- Practice it often during the day. If it is inconvenient to lie down, you can do this also while sitting or standing. Concentrate on your abdomen moving up and down, the air moving in and out of your lungs, and the feeling of relaxation that deep breathing gives you.

- Do a set of six to twelve deep breaths.

*How does this feel? Are there any difficulties?*

_____

_____

_____

## Biblical Meditation

Meditation is a form of mind exercise used to self-regulate one's thoughts and feelings. There are many different types of meditation, many of which originate from ancient times. Among numerous findings regarding its positive benefits to physical and mental health, meditation has been demonstrated to reduce anxiety, depression, and negative emotions, and increase self-awareness, learning, and memory.[5] It can clear your mind from information overload that builds throughout the day to bring calm and peace.

Here we will focus on biblical meditation, which draws our attention away from the world and ourselves, and directs it to God. The book of Psalms is full of references to meditate on God's love, faithfulness, and creation: "We meditate on your unfailing love" (Psalm 48:9). When we do this, we are more likely to feel God's presence, which engenders peace, comfort, and joy. In other passages of the Bible, we are encouraged to meditate on God's laws, which help us to be "prosperous and successful."[6]

*Practice biblical meditation by yourself and with your clients:*

- Focus your attention on a Bible verse or passage that brings comfort, peace, and hope to your client.

- Find a comfortable position.

- Breathe deeply to calm your mind and heart as shown above.

- Spend 15-20 minutes on the biblical passage you have chosen with your client. You may read it or recite it to him from memory or have him speak it if he has memorized it.

*Pick one biblical passage that you can use to start your meditation:*

_____

_____

_____

_____

_____

## Guided Imagery

Guided imagery uses all of our senses to focus and direct our thoughts and feelings to provide relaxation and relief from the effects of distress. Research has established its positive impact on mental and physical health as well as performance.[7] For example, imagining a perfect piano recital can help enhance one's actual performance. As little as 10 minutes of guided imagery has been shown to reduce blood pressure, lower cholesterol and glucose levels in the blood, and increase short-term immune cell activity. It can also reduce post-surgery morphine use, lessen headaches, and decrease general pain. Guided imagery can decrease symptoms of anxiety and depression. You can invent your own or use someone else's imagery.

*Practice guided imagery by yourself and with your clients:*

- Take a few minutes to imagine something you did in the past that you found enjoyable, or some place that makes you feel happy, relaxed, peaceful, and safe.

- Example: A special place might be at the end of a path that leads to a lake. Grass is under your feet, the lake is about 30 yards away, and mountains are in the distance. You can feel the coolness of the air in this shady spot. The birds are chirping. The sun is bright on the pond. You can feel the warmth of the sun on your back. The smell of jasmine is in the air.

- Example: Your special place might be a sparkling clean kitchen, with cinnamon rolls baking in the oven. You can smell the aroma of the bread baking. Through the kitchen window you can see your garden filled with bright bursts of color from your favorite flowers. A window chime flutters in the breeze. There is a cup of tea for yourself on the table – an invitation for you to sit and relax.

- In any image that you create, you can picture Jesus being with you to heal, restore, and give you rest.

- Go through your image:

  Close your eyes. As you count from 1 to 5, you will become more and more relaxed. 1... You are relaxed. 2...You are safe. 3...You are comfortable. 4...You are at peace. 5... Walk slowly to a quiet, serene place in your mind. What do you see? Smell? Hear? Notice what is before you. Reach out and touch it. Sit or lie down in your special place. How does it feel? Make the temperature comfortable. Feel the ground with your feet. Look above you. This is your place and nothing can harm you here. Spend a few minutes realizing that you are relaxed, safe, and comfortable. Memorize this place's smells, tastes, sights, and sounds. You can come back and relax here whenever you want. Leave by the same path or entrance. You can count backwards from 5 to 1. 5...You are relaxed. 4... 3...You feel calm. 2... 1...You are alert and refreshed. Open your eyes.

*Write down your peaceful, happy place (make sure to describe what you see, hear, smell, taste, and touch):*

_____

_____

_____

_____

_____

_____

## Journaling

We are all familiar with the concept of writing in a diary. Journaling is somewhat like this, except that it is more flexible, and it focuses on understanding our thoughts and feelings more than reporting of the day's events. You can journal about interactions you have had, upcoming events that are causing you stress, how you feel about something, etc. Much evidence exists to support the use of journaling to decrease distress:[8]

- Cognitively: The act of writing accesses your left brain, which is analytical and rational. This can help clarify your thoughts and feelings, better understand what is happening, and solve problems more effectively.

- Emotionally: Writing about distressing events helps you to come to terms with them, thus reducing the impact of these stressors on your emotional health. When you write about situations that cause you to feel sad or angry, it can release the intensity of these feelings. By doing this, you will feel calmer and more at peace.

- Physically: Regular journaling strengthens immune cells, decreases symptoms of asthma, and reduces rheumatoid arthritis, among other diseases.

I would like to invite you to journal. It will help you to be healthier, and the healthier you are, the more internal resources you have to help someone else. Get a journal or write on a password-protected account. Write about anything, in what I call "stream of consciousness," i.e., whatever comes to mind with no regard for grammar or for anyone else reading what you have written. It is important not to censor what you write to get the full benefit of journaling. Invite your clients to do the same. In addition, you can ask your clients to bring in their journals to share with you – if they wish and believe that it will be helpful to the work you are doing together.

*Do you have any concerns about journaling?*

_____

_____

_____

## Cognitive Restructuring

We are made up of our thoughts, feelings, and behaviors. They are interrelated and can impact one another. What we think has an impact on how we feel and what we do.

Imagine that you are driving, and someone abruptly cuts into your lane without any warning. Honestly, what do you think? How do you feel? What would you do? When you do not have full, accurate knowledge of what, why, and how this just happened, many of you will automatically judge him to be a terrible driver, feel irritated, and then even honk or gesture to let him know how you feel. What if I were to tell you that the person is on his way to the hospital, because he just got a call that his daughter was in a terrible accident and was taken via ambulance to the ER. Does this change what you think? And then does this change how you feel and what you do? With this added information, your internal experience might change to better fit the situation: You might feel less annoyed, more compassionate, and then perhaps even move out of the way so that he can get to the hospital sooner.

Life presents situations, such as the one above, that can be experienced in different ways. It is important to your mental health to be more aware of your negative thoughts, and exercise other ways of processing information to facilitate more constructive feelings and behaviors. Cognitive restructuring is the process of learning to be aware of one's faulty thoughts, challenging them, and then substituting them for more reality-based, accurate, and adaptive thinking. It has been demonstrated to have helpful effects on people suffering from various physical and mental health issues.[9] Some of the common cognitive distortions include:

- All/None: Thinking in absolute, uncompromising, extreme terms – "If you aren't going to do it perfectly, don't do it at all."

- Overgeneralization: Taking an isolated incident and using it to conclude something that is beyond the facts – "You are never there for me."

- Jumping to Conclusions: Drawing usually negative conclusions based on little to no evidence – You ask a question and your teenager does not answer, you then think, "He's disrespecting me."

- Demanding/Coercive Statements: This is the tendency to make your wants into demands for yourself or the rest of the world – "You should do it this way."

- Categorical Thinking: Rather than describing the specific behaviors, you assign a label that makes the behavior the whole of the individual – "You are worthless."

- Personalization: Taking personal responsibility for situations that are not within one's control – "Everything is my fault."

*Which irrational, maladaptive thoughts are you most likely to engage in?*

_____

_____

_____

_____

*Practice cognitive restructuring using the table at the end of this session.*

### Role-Playing

This is a therapeutic tool that is used to increase our understanding of another person's perspective by putting ourselves in that person's place. It is also a way of preparing ourselves to confront issues with another, particularly when we do not want to communicate our thoughts and feelings to the other for fear of his anger, rejection, and/or judgment.

Here is an example of a role-play: Your client reports that she is having difficulty with someone in her church. The situation has deteriorated to the extent that she no longer wants to attend church. When you explore the possibility of discussing the situation with that person in accordance with Matthew 18, she has been afraid to do so.[10] At this point, it might be beneficial to role-play the possible dialogues she can have with that person with you. She can be herself and you can take on the role of the other person, and the two of you can explore various ways in which the conversation can proceed. Alternately, you can portray her while she plays the other. Either way, role-play may increase her understanding of the issues between them, sympathy for the other person's position, and confidence in herself to confront the situation.

*Choose a partner in the training group and role-play the above scenario. You can create the specific issue together, and then, take turns being the protagonist and the antagonist.*

## Using Media

Books, movies, and television shows depict universal themes that we find poignant, entertaining, and inspiring. These can be helpful in decreasing a sense of being alone with one's struggles, present alternate ways of looking at situations, reduce denial with regard to challenges, increase emotional expression, engender hope, and facilitate change.[11] You can suggest a specific book, movie, or show, based on what is appropriate for your client. It is imperative that your client is ready to delve into the issues portrayed in the media you choose. Make sure you have read or seen what you are recommending and that you are prepared to discuss the effects on your client.

Here are a few examples:

- If you have a client who is struggling with self- and other-condemnation, you might advise reading Philip Yancey's *What's So Amazing About Grace?*

- If you are with a client who is in turmoil due to having a family member who is struggling with psychosis, you might suggest watching *A Beautiful Mind*.

- If you are working with a client who suffers from obsessive compulsive disorder, you might propose watching the television series, *Monk*.

*List some books/movies/television programs that you can use with your clients and why these would be helpful in counseling:*

_____

_____

_____

_____

_____

_____

The therapeutic techniques we covered in this session are helpful for you as you seek to increase your own mental and physical health. Some of you may find it easy to practice them, while others of you may find yourself resisting in applying these in your lives. If the latter is the case, pay attention to what you are thinking and feeling about these tools, and work to overcome any reservations you have about them. This will aid in dealing with possible obstacles you will face when you counsel others to apply them. It is important to become proficient in these tools in order to train others to use them.

**Thought Record**

| Negative Thought | Evidence in Support of That Thought | Evidence Against That Thought | Alternative Thought |
|---|---|---|---|
| He doesn't like me. | He didn't say anything when I said, "Hi." | He has invited me over to his home before. | He didn't see/hear me. |
|  |  |  |  |
|  |  |  |  |
|  |  |  |  |
|  |  |  |  |
|  |  |  |  |

# Session 4

## Types of Counseling Formats

Religious leaders of Jesus' day separated themselves and kept their distance from those they considered to be "sinners" for fear of being contaminated. They considered many to be inferior and prided themselves on being holy.[1] The people that they disdained were those who were suffering mental, physical, and spiritual anguish. In contrast, Jesus consistently drew near to these individuals to comfort and heal them.[2]

On many occasions, Jesus approaches individuals, one-on-one. One of the most memorable interchanges in the Bible occurs when Jesus initiates a conversation with a Samaritan woman.[3] I imagine that she has suffered much: She appears to have been rejected and abandoned by five men as well as the women in her town (as observed by her coming to the well to draw water by herself at that time of the day). She is currently living with a man who is not her husband, which is considered to be a sexually immoral behavior. Instead of condemning and distancing himself from her as the Pharisees would have done, Jesus talks with her as He does anyone else, helps her understand that she is known and accepted by Him, and invites her to be saved by drinking the "living water" that only He can give. Her life is changed as a result of this encounter with Jesus.

Not only an individual's life but also families' lives are changed as a result of being with Jesus. One familiar account involves the family of Mary, Martha, and Lazarus.[4] It is clear that these siblings have a special relationship with Jesus. When Lazarus is sick, Mary and Martha reach out to Jesus. When he dies, they are honest in their lament to Him. Jesus exhibits compassion and love for this family, and ultimately, manifests God's glory by bringing Lazarus back to life. What is a cause for grief and mourning now turns into joy and celebration. This family's life is transformed by the love of Jesus.

Jesus also often interacts with groups. Yet another well-known story involves five loaves of bread and two fish.[5] In this particular event, a large crowd follows Jesus, and He is moved to help them. Eventually, disciples begin to wonder how they are going to feed all the people and arrive at a solution of sending them away to fend for themselves. However, Jesus uses what He finds, five loaves and two fish, and multiplies them exponentially to feed everyone. The crowd experiences a miracle through Jesus, and is enriched — physically, emotionally, and spiritually.

In all the above stories, Jesus recognizes and fulfills people's needs, e.g., for food, healing, acceptance, love, and life. We observe how Jesus is able to relate to individuals, families, and groups to meet them where they are. While we cannot be Jesus, we can try to follow His example in the various ways God brings people to us.

## Meeting with an Individual

This is probably the most frequent and least complicated type of lay counseling you will do. This format is best if your client has an issue that only affects himself and does not include anyone else in his family. An example would be someone who is relatively functional who recently has had a conflict at work that he needs help to resolve. The main goal here is to understand his concerns and explore options for what he can do to rectify his work situation.

Sometimes, your client's problems may involve others in the family, but no one else is willing to be part of getting help, in which case, the one person who is willing to work on the issues will begin individual counseling. This is not ideal; however, even by one person thinking, feeling, or doing things differently, the others in the family may be positively affected to change. For example, there is a conflict in the home between a father and his son, but the mother comes in for counseling. By changing her attitudes and behaviors toward her husband and her son, e.g., she no longer triangulates one when she has issues with the other, this will impact how the other two relate to one another.

The nature of the concerns also has a bearing on the type of counseling format needed. Challenges, such as social anxiety, depression, low self-esteem, addictions, post-traumatic stress, and anger management, can be effectively treated through individual meetings. Clearly, the more severe issues are beyond the scope of lay counseling and need to be referred to a professional mental health provider. We will cover the referral process more specifically in a later session.

One logistical comment: Usually, it is prudent to match the counselor with a client who is of the same gender in order to avoid any perception of improprieties. In addition, many may prefer counselors of the same gender as they may regard them to be more understanding of what they are experiencing given the common ground they have in being a woman/wife/mom/daughter or man/husband/dad/son. Even if this is not the case, and the client wishes to meet with a counselor of the opposite gender, keeping to the same gender rule might still be helpful in terms of working through preconceived notions that are interfering with feeling comfortable with a counselor of the same gender.

### A Note on Children & Adolescents

Additional information to keep in mind when counseling minors (some of this will be covered in more detail when we discuss legal and ethical issues in lay counseling in a later session):

- Make sure you have permission from both parents to meet with their child(ren).

- Instead of sitting in an office and engaging just verbally, you might consider walking together, playing a game, and going to a park with your child clients.

- Reflect their ways of communicating, e.g., do not be too formal in your approach with kids.

- Use words that are commensurate with your client's developmental level.

*Imagine you are an individual client seeking help: What kind of lay counselor would you want?*

_____

_____

_____

_____

## Meeting with Couples

There are couples in the church who are constantly at war with one another – in obvious and subtle ways. They seem unable to resolve their negative thoughts and feelings about one another and their relationship without intervention. As the first step in restoring their relationship, it might be beneficial for them to be seen by lay counselors who can provide a safe place to face one another, communicate their viewpoints, and emphasize their strengths to overcome their areas of difficulties.

Rather than seeing a counselor on an individual basis, it is more effective to work on their relational issues together. When you only work with one partner around a marital issue, you miss important information about the other partner and their relationship. For example, your observation of your client is that she is smart, considerate, and lovely, and thus, you cannot understand how her husband is not supportive of her. You then meet them together, and realize that she does not respond to him in ways that she responds to you; in fact, you observe that she is constantly disrespectful of him, which is a significant contributing factor in how he treats her. Had you continued to only see the wife, you would have been working under a false paradigm that she has created (sometimes unconsciously), contributing to a counseling experience that may not be successful in repairing your client's relationship.

In addition, it is optimal to have couples meet with a lay counseling pair who is also a couple. This usually does not occur in the professional mental health practices due to the high cost of paying two providers to be present at the same time and limited availability of two therapists who are a couple. Lay counseling then can provide a service where a couple trained together in this ministry can meet with another couple struggling with their relationship. Once it is set up this way, I do not advise "one-on-one" meetings where the husband client-counselor dyad meets separately from the wife client-counselor dyad. This becomes too often a complaining session about the spouse who is not present. This can lead to one feeling more accepted and the other feeling more alienated. Sometimes, meeting separately also leads to one dyad meeting more often to work on the marital issues than the other dyad: This can create resentment, hurt, and anger at the perceived imbalance of investment in the relationship. Thus, I recommend that all meetings take place with the four – one pair as the counselor and other pair as the client – together.

### A Note on Children & Adolescents

This seems obvious and should go without saying, however, in some situations this does occur, and thus, needs to be addressed: Sometimes, couples will bring their kids to their counseling meetings due to lack of child care and expect them to sit quietly doing a task (e.g., watching a movie with headphones, playing on the computer or reading). While I can understand that it may be convenient to bring one's kids, it has a negative effect on the kids' sense of emotional security and safety to be exposed to their parents' issues in detail. It also inhibits the couples from being free and honest to share whatever they need to in order to do the necessary work to heal and restore their relationship.

*What do you think would be especially difficult for you in working with couples?*

_____

_____

_____

_____

## Meeting with Families

A family is a system with its own unique personality that profoundly affects its members. It has well-established principles and patterns, such as, prayers before bedtime, picking up after oneself, respecting each other's privacy, yelling or being silent when things do not go according to one's expectations, only highlighting mistakes to be corrected, and being allies against the identified problem child or parent. Some of these rules and values are beneficial to maintaining healthy relationships while others are not. It is in the latter cases that families might need outside assistance.

Desmond Tutu, a South African activist and a retired Anglican bishop once stated, "You don't choose your family. They are God's gift to you, as you are to them." Unfortunately, many people do not experience their families as gifts from God, rather they consider their families as entities to be avoided due to the high levels of stress they experience when they are together. Instead of feeling encouraged and supported, one's family can be associated with pain and suffering. Some struggle with feeling like they are not good enough for their families – that they are not a blessing but an embarrassment. Somehow, they think that they do not fit in with other members of their family that they perceive to be smarter, prettier, and nicer.

In many cases, an individual's difficulties stem from what is occurring in one's family. For example, a child who has been an excellent student may suddenly do poorly in school due to being anxious over having a parent who has just been diagnosed with cancer. Meeting with the child alone to do better in school may not fully address his problems. Instead, it is beneficial to meet together as a family to discuss how this crisis is affecting everyone and how each member of the family is coping with it. By meeting the whole family, you have a better understanding of the situation, and therefore, can devise more effective approaches for helping the family to function in healthier ways.

### A Note on Children & Adolescents

An additional factor to consider when meeting with families where children are involved: It is important to respect their perspectives and take them into account. Many cultures have a history of keeping children silent ("Kids should be seen and not heard"), but this is not conducive to facilitating healthy interchanges in families. And when you are exploring the situation with the kids in the family, do not set up the conversation in ways that would make them have to choose one parent over another (e.g., "Who do you think is right, your mom or dad?"). Instead, invite their input through more general open-ended questions (e.g., "What is your opinion about this?").

*Reflect on your family-of-origin and then on your immediate family. In general, are they a cause for joy? Or suffering? In what ways?*

_____

_____

_____

_____

_____

_____

## Meeting in Support Groups

While it is helpful to have small groups based on physical proximity, developmental stage in life, and/or interests, it is also valuable to have support groups based on mental health related issues. It can be daunting to go to a professional due to unfamiliarity, cost, and stigma inherent in this process. Instead, church members can attend small groups where they can share common concerns, give and receive encouragement, and move forward together. There is a sense of relief and connection that comes from being together with others who are struggling in similar ways. Examples of concerns that support groups in churches can address are as follows:

- Parenting Children/Teenagers

- Coping with Special Needs Child

- Dealing with Losses

- Managing Chronic Pain

- Caring for Non-Christian Family Member(s)

- People in Recovery from Addictions

- Coping with Depression/Anxiety/Mental Disorders

- Taking Care of Aging Parents

- Stress Management

Lay counselors can facilitate these groups alone or in pairs. In choosing a particular issue to begin a support group, it is helpful if the lay counselors have had some personal experiences that they have overcome in that area. The following are some additional factors to consider in creating a group:

- Commitment: In order for a group to be healthy, it is important for group members to value and respect the group and its members. One essential factor in demonstrating this: attendance. Make sure that you contract with each member to commit to the group by attending consistently.

- Open/Closed: Decide whether you want to leave the group open for individuals to join anytime or you want to have set times in which people can join the group. In the latter case, you begin and stay with the same members throughout the time that you run the group.

- Limited/Indefinite Time Frame: Groups can have a certain length of time that they meet. Alternatively, groups can meet on a long-term basis with no definite end period. How you decide this depends on the nature of the issue, e.g., a group to comfort chronic pain sufferers may work best to meet for an indefinite period of time while a group to console those who have lost a loved one to cancer may work best to meet for a specified period of time.

- Structured/Unstructured Format: Prior to beginning a group, decide whether you want to use a tool, such as a book or a video series, to facilitate your discussions. Alternatively, you can have an unstructured group where you allow members to bring in thoughts and feelings that they have experienced throughout the week, and the group can provide support around these concerns.

- Approach: Use what you learn in this curriculum to discuss various issues. Inform the group members to keep everything confidential, listen to one another, share only about themselves and their concerns (not about others outside the group), and offer encouragement toward positive changes.

- Logistics: Choose how many people you want in your group. Six to eight is optimal. You can meet on a weekly, bi-weekly, or monthly basis for one to two hours. Decide your preferences depending on the flexibility of the group members, and urgency and nature of the issues you will be discussing in the group. Also, consider serving refreshments as this can result in a sense of congeniality, affection, and openness that are conducive to a positive group experience.

### A Note on Children &Adolescents

Support groups can be a powerful tool in producing positive changes in children and adolescents. In general, kids are more vulnerable to being self-conscious, to peer influences, and to feeling alone in their struggles, than adults. Being in a group with other kids who are struggling in similar fashion may help them in ways that meeting in individual or family formats will not. They may learn to overcome their self-consciousness better as they observe others, who are like them, work through this. Their peers' constructive feedback is understood and applied more quickly than adults' input, particularly for teenagers. And certainly, they will not feel so alone as they realize that other kids are facing comparable challenges in their lives.

The following is a list of possible topics for kids' groups:

- Separation in the Family

- Identity Exploration

- Balancing Academic, Social, and Parental Expectations

- Social Skills

- Teen Issues[6]

*What are some groups you would be interested in facilitating? Why?*

_____

_____

_____


*How would you begin a new group in your church?*

_____

_____

_____


You can meet with people in various configurations depending on the nature of the problem; the openness, willingness, and availability of the people involved; and the purpose for which they are seeking help. During your initial contact, determine which format you want to use and ask whether that would be acceptable to your client. Also consider the possibility of your client engaging in multiple counseling formats at the same time, i.e., your client can meet with you one-on-one and also attend a support group. This can lead to a quicker resolution of issues in some cases. Decide on the best strategy together with your client.

# Session 5

## Regarding Mental Health

As you work in this lay counseling ministry, it is important to understand what mental health is, where you stand in terms of your own mental health, and how to encourage yourself and others toward greater mental health. So, what does it mean to be mentally healthy?

### State of Well-Being

World Health Organization defines mental health as "a state of well-being in which every individual realizes his or her own potential, can cope with the normal stresses of life, can work productively and fruitfully, and is able to make a contribution to her or his community."[1]

*Given the above definition, are you mentally healthy? Give examples to support your answer:*

_____

_____

_____

_____

## Self-Awareness, Self-Acceptance, and Self-Esteem

A state of well-being begins with self-awareness, self-acceptance, and self-esteem. At its quintessential level, self-awareness refers to recognizing yourself as being separate and different from others. It also means having an understanding of your own thoughts, feelings, and character. These are some of the questions you can contemplate as you increase your self-awareness: Who am I? What do I like? What makes me afraid? Whom do I admire and why?

Once you know yourself, it is important to accept yourself as you are. This means that you acknowledge your positive characteristics without fanfare. In addition, rather than deny or minimize your flaws, examine them and reconcile yourself to being imperfect in certain ways.

Once you accept yourself, you can then begin changing to better reflect God. It is a paradoxical truth that you cannot change for the better if you do not accept who you are first. When you are able to acknowledge yourself in positive and negative ways, then you are also able to work toward building a healthy sense of self-worth. This then positively influences how you are in the world, and more specifically, how well you relate to others. Having self-respect, confidence, and self-love – which are all characteristics of self-esteem – help you to function in healthy ways and equip you to help others.

*How would you describe yourself?*

_____

_____

_____

*What are some of your faults that you find difficult to accept?*

_____

_____

_____

*On a scale of 1-10 (with "1" being extremely low to "10" being extremely high), how would you rate your self-esteem? What has contributed to this?*

_____

_____

_____

_____

## Passions, Talents, and Purpose

Another characteristic of mental health is realizing one's potential. When we gaze at a baby, we like to project onto them endless possibilities of who she will become and what she will accomplish. As babies grow from being toddlers to teenagers to adults, their potential becomes more circumscribed by their passions, talents, and purpose in life. It is critical to know what interests you have in order to forge a path toward a meaningful future. What grabs your attention? What do you feel intensely about?

Since you are in this lay counseling training, I suspect that one of your passions is helping people who are in mental and emotional distress. In addition to identifying what you are enthusiastic about, it is also important to recognize what you are good at. With which talents and gifts has God blessed you? Perhaps you are athletic, musically inclined, creative, empathetic, discerning, etc. Again, given that you are taking this course, I imagine that you have the gifts of encouragement, mercy, leadership, and/or wisdom. It is not enough just to recognize your passions and talents. You need to bring them together to realize your potential and move toward living a meaningful, purposeful life.

*What are your passions?*

_____

_____

_____

*What are your talents and gifts?*

_____

_____

_____

*What is the purpose for your life, and how are you on track for achieving this?*

_____

_____

_____

## Coping with Stressors

Those who are mentally healthy use adaptive strategies to cope with stressors. In order to be able to do this, you first have to recognize stressors as they occur and acknowledge how these challenging situations impact your internal and external systems. Stress occurs as a response to anticipatory events and to actual incidents that disturb one's normal equilibrium, e.g., illnesses, accidents, and dealing with hostile people.

Many people manifest tension through physical symptoms, such as, headaches, intestinal problems, muscle tension, and back pain. Others know they are troubled because of behavioral changes, such as, withdrawing from people, procrastinating on tasks, eating too much, and sleeping more than usual. Stress affects cognitive functioning as well: You might experience impaired concentration, increased distractibility, and more thought distortions. There are also emotional indications that one is under pressure, e.g., feeling overwhelmed, anxious, irritated, restless, and impatient.

Once you become aware of when and how stress affects you, it is important to learn how to manage it well. In addition to the tools mentioned in session three, incorporate the following to your repertoire of positive coping strategies: exercise, appropriate boundaries with people and work, sharing your difficulties with others, and taking time to laugh.

*What makes you stressed?*

_____

_____

_____

*How do you know you are stressed?*

_____

_____

_____

*How do you cope with your stressors?*

_____

_____

_____

## Working Productively and Fruitfully

Working productively and fruitfully is another characteristic of feeling content with oneself and one's life. Just working endlessly is not the goal, because, in the long run, this results in inefficient process, ineffective output, and burnout. We have a plum tree in our backyard that has yielded delicious plums each year. Last year, it produced so much fruit that we were able to give away about 50 bags with 30-40 plums each. My family, friends, and I were looking forward to eating these plums again this year, but for the first time in 12 years, our tree did not bear any fruit at all. After some research, we found that a number of tree species can become alternate bearing: If they yield a heavy crop one year, they will produce little or no fruit the following year. While there are various factors involved in this phenomenon, two of the major causes of alternate bearing are age and excessively heavy yield the previous year. Every year that our plum tree yielded more and more fruit, we were delighted to eat them and give them away, not realizing that our fruit tree would eventually need to rest in order to thrive again. Similarly, people also need to balance work and relaxation in order to be productive and fruitful, which is necessary for mental health.

*What do you spend most of your time working on?*

_____

_____

_____

*What are the fruits of your labors?*

_____

_____

_____

*How do you balance work and leisure time?*

_____

_____

_____

## Contributing to Our Community

Whatever work you do, if you frame it in terms of how your work benefits people, organizations, and/or societies, you will feel better about yourself and your life. For example, if you are a public defender who works with criminals who cannot afford to hire a private attorney, you might spend much of your time being with people you do not like, examining the evidence in ways you are not particularly proud of in order to most effectively defend your client. While trying to understand that which is personally incomprehensible, you must also guard against attacks by the public and law enforcement personnel for the work you do. At times, you might feel inconsequential, depressed, guilty, and trapped, which obviously are not signs of positive mental health. Instead of thinking of your job in these ways, consider it an essential work that contributes to the justice system, and that because of what you do, there are innocent people who are experiencing a fair trial and are not unfairly imprisoned. Framing your job in this way will increase the likelihood that you feel a sense of self-worth and life satisfaction, which lead to experiencing greater mental health.

Another form of work is volunteering our resources: time, energy, money, and/or expertise. A common trait found in those who are mentally healthy is that they selflessly contribute to their community. The relationship between health and volunteer work has been studied extensively, and the general conclusion is that when you volunteer, you are physically and psychologically healthier. One study found that volunteering is correlated with happiness, life satisfaction, self-esteem, a sense of control over one's life, and physical health.[2] Thus, contributing to our community is one of the keys to unlocking the mental health code.

*How do you volunteer your resources for your community?*

_____

_____

_____

After studying the above dimensions of mental health, how would you now answer the initial question, *Are you mentally healthy?* As you work to strengthen your health, you can more effectively help others to improve theirs. When you meet with your clients, review the above criteria for being mentally fit and assess where they are doing well and where they need to change. We can also learn from and follow someone in history who epitomizes mental health – Jesus.

## Jesus: Personification of Mental Health

When we read the Gospels, it is clear that Jesus models what it means to be in a state of well-being. He is definitely aware of who He is – the Son of God and Son of Man. He is comfortable with Himself: He is not driven by public opinion. He is secure, stable, and grounded in God's love and calling. Jesus realizes and fulfills His life's purpose – to teach, heal, serve, and ultimately give his life for us so that we may have an eternal relationship with God. Jesus also has suffered the stresses of life. Like us, He has been tempted, moved to intense emotions of grief and anger, and misunderstood by many who do not understand who He is and what He is doing. He copes with these difficult moments with strength and grace, and in keeping with God's will for His life. He works productively and fruitfully by meeting people's needs wherever He goes: feeding the hungry, healing the sick, teaching truths, and helping people to experience life in a way they never had before. As we look at Jesus' life, we see someone who has not only contributed to the world but also fundamentally changed it. In every way, He fits the definition of mental health.

*Consider how Jesus can or has changed your life to reflect mental health:*

_____

_____

_____

_____

_____

_____

## Concerning Mental Health Issues

For the next six sessions, we will focus on various mental health issues that you might find in the church members who seek lay counseling. Usually people request help when they are in a crisis that exceeds their capacity to cope. In some cases, there is impairment in cognitive, emotional, and behavioral aspects of their lives. In severe instances, their distress may significantly interfere with their ability to function normally. For example, a student might not be able to go to school due to being extremely anxious and/or depressed.

Mental health and disorders fall on a continuum from normal to abnormal. From time to time, we have all experienced dysfunctional symptoms. For example, if you have been in a car accident where someone suddenly crashed into your car, you might be very nervous about driving and even avoid driving immediately thereafter. And when you drive again, you might be more inclined to check the mirrors more frequently to try to anticipate possible drivers or cars that might pose a danger to you. This is a natural reaction to a trauma and may last several days or weeks. The difference between a diagnosable mental illness and a natural repercussion of an event involves taking into account the duration, frequency, number of symptoms, and severity of the disability. In the above situation, if after the accident, you are no longer able to drive or if you continue to experience extreme anxiety whenever you are in the car for fear of someone colliding into your car, and these kinds of symptoms last months or years, then it is no longer a natural, normal reaction but a mental disorder.

Mental illnesses are diagnosed by various mental health professionals: psychologists, psychiatrists, marriage and family therapists (MFT), and licensed clinical social workers (LCSW). If you suspect that the individuals you are counseling suffer from mental disorders, please refer them to one of the above providers. We will discuss the referral process in more depth in a later session. In your capacity as a lay counselor, focus on encouraging people to engage in practices that engender mental health, particularly as described above and as manifested in Jesus.

# Session 6

## Depressive and Anxiety Disorders

What do you think is the most frequent command in the Bible? "Love one another." "Be good." "Do not sin." None of these. The most repeated command in the Bible is, "Do not fear."[1] God knows our hearts and minds, and speaks to how all of us can be anxious and afraid. God usually follows this command with a reassurance that He is always with us.[2]

While the Bible does not use the word, "depression," there are often references to people, like Job and David, who have been troubled by sadness, discouragement, anguish, and despair. Jesus, having allowed Himself to be fully human, also has experienced moments of fear and anguish, particularly as He faced the cross. Thus, Jesus perfectly understands and walks with us when we are in these emotional places of pain.

*Read Luke 12:22-34. What are your thoughts and feelings about Jesus' words?*

_____

_____

_____

_____

*What are the implications for you and your work as a lay counselor?*

_____

_____

_____

_____

## Diagnostic and Statistical Manual of Mental Disorders (DSM-5)

Mental health professionals use DSM-5 to diagnose various conditions.[3] It classifies all mental disorders and provides a common language for mental health providers to be used for assessment, treatment, and payment for mental health services. What people customarily refer to as depression and anxiety are broad categories that consist of multiple disorders.

Depressive disorders include the following: disruptive mood dysregulation disorder, major depressive disorder, dysthymia, premenstrual dysphoric disorder, and substance/ medication-induced depressive disorder. Each of these has its own specific symptom checklist, with differing prevalence, development, and prognosis, among other factors. What they all have in common is disruption in mood to such an extent that it interferes significantly with social, occupational, and other areas of life.

Anxiety disorders include the following: separation anxiety disorder, selective mutism, specific phobia, social anxiety disorder, panic disorder, agoraphobia, generalized anxiety disorder, substance/medication-induced anxiety disorder. Like the depressive disorders, each of these has its own particular diagnostic features, prevalence rates, risk factors, and course of illness, among other variables. The underlying thread that holds these disorders together is excessive fear or anxiety of what is perceived as a threat to one's well-being. These interfere with normal functioning in various ways.

For our purposes, it is unnecessary to study in detail the specific disorders. However, it is important to have a general understanding of the above two classifications – depressive and anxiety disorders – as they include the most frequent conditions we will encounter in the church as well as in our other communities.

## Depressive Disorders

World Health Organization estimates that 350 million people suffer from depression globally.[4] Approximately 10% of the U.S. adult population exhibit some form of depressive disorders.[5] Women are 1.5 to 3 times more likely to experience depression than men. Average age in which disorder emerges is at 32, although it is possible at any age, particularly during adolescence, for symptoms to manifest.

Basically, depression involves having either a depressed mood (which is indicated by feelings of sadness, emptiness, and hopelessness) or loss of interest in previously pleasurable activities for a certain length of time on a consistent basis. Some of the symptoms include sleep disturbance, weight gain/loss, fatigue, feeling of worthlessness, decreased ability to concentrate, and suicidal thoughts.

What causes someone to be depressed? Childhood trauma, stressful life events, and negative temperament all increase the likelihood of the onset of depression. In addition, if you have family members who are diagnosed with some type of depression, you are two to four times more likely to be at risk for a depressive disorder than those who do not. Furthermore, if one is suffering from any other disorders – anxiety, substance use, personality disorders, and chronic illnesses – one is also more likely to be depressed.

Some individuals with depression can function relatively well, with symptoms that are so mild that others are unaware that anything is wrong. Other individuals can be incapacitated to such an extent that they cannot attend to basic hygiene needs or leave their beds. Most suffer from depression in between these two limits. They tend to function at a less than optimal level, with effects, such as, immune suppression, decreased social functioning, and impaired mental acuity.

Treatments for depressive disorders include individual and group psychotherapy, and medication. There is evidence that alternative remedies, such as, bright light therapy, exercise, herbal supplements, meditation, yoga, guided imagery, and aromatherapy might be helpful in coping with depression.

*Have you ever had any of the following symptoms? Please check any of the symptoms that apply to you. This checklist is not to be used to diagnose yourself or anyone else (only mental health professionals can assess accurately). Instead, use it to increase your understanding of depressive disorders.*

☐  Sadness

☐  Emptiness

☐  Hopelessness

☐  Irritability

☐  Loss of interest or pleasure in most activities

☐  Excessive guilt

☐  Significant weight gain or loss

☐  Insomnia or hypersomnia

☐  Feeling of restlessness or being slowed down

☐  Fatigue

☐  Diminished ability to concentrate

☐  Suicidal thoughts

*If you endorsed any of the above indicators, what caused you to experience those?*

_____

_____

_____

*How did you manage the above symptoms?*

_____

_____

_____

_____

*Would you deal with them differently now? If yes, how?*

_____

_____

_____

_____

## Suicide

People who are depressed are at higher risk for suicide. Other risk factors include past history of suicidal thoughts/attempts, being male, living alone, and feeling hopeless. Suicide is a desperate behavior to stop one's pain and suffering. Many turn to suicide, because it feels like it is the only way to escape their intolerable situation. There are other options, but due to their feelings of despair and hopelessness, they cannot see them.

There were over 38,000 suicides in the US in 2010: Someone died via suicide every 13.7 minutes.[6] Centers for Disease Control and Prevention (CDC) report that, from 1999-2010, there was a 28% increase of suicides for 35-64 year olds. The greatest increase of suicide rates (49%) was among the 50-59 year olds. In 2010, an estimated 12 suicide attempts occurred per every completed suicide, as observed in hospital visits from people with self-inflicted injuries who survived their suicide attempts. Although women are two to three times more likely to attempt suicide, men are four times more likely to die from suicide than women.

The following are warning signs for suicide:

- Depression and other mental disorders

- Social isolation

- Family history of mental disorder or substance abuse

- Family violence, including physical or sexual abuse

- Preoccupation with death

- Hopelessness

- Suicide plan

- Having the means to commit suicide

- Previous suicide attempt(s)

If you or someone you know is in danger of attempting suicide, it is crucial to seek professional help. Treatments for people who are at risk for suicide include psychotherapy, medication, and inpatient hospitalization.

**Anxiety Disorders**

Anxiety can be a normal response to life experiences as it protects us from potentially harmful elements in our environment. For example, having an apprehension about strangers reduces the likelihood that you will be harmed. Anxiety also serves a positive purpose in performance. Some amount of anxiety or stress fuels our motivation and energy to accomplish our tasks well. However, a high degree of anxiety can impair one's daily functioning.

Anxiety disorders are the most common mental illness in the U.S. National Institute of Mental Health reports that 40 million adults in the U.S. (18.1%) experience some form of anxiety disorder in a 12-month period.[7] In general, women are 60% more likely to experience an anxiety disorder over their lifetime than men. It is more likely that 30-44 year olds will develop a form of anxiety disorder than any other age group. 8% of adolescents (13-18) have an anxiety disorder, with the first symptoms observed at around age six.

Essentially, an anxiety disorder involves excessive anxiety or fear about a situation or object. Psychologists distinguish between the states of fear and anxiety: Fear is a response to real or perceived immediate danger in which the sympathetic nervous system is activated to allow one to fight or flee, while anxiety is a response to anticipation of future danger and is linked to vigilance, cautious behaviors, and muscle tension. The individual suffering from an anxiety disorder finds it difficult to control his worries or panic, and either actively avoids or endures the feared object or situation with intense distress. This causes significant distress and disrupts one's life in various areas of functioning.

What causes someone to be excessively anxious or fearful? Negative temperament, behavioral inhibition, childhood trauma, and parental overprotectiveness are all risk factors for the development of an anxiety disorder. In addition, genetic variables can influence the manifestation of most of the anxiety disorders. For example, social anxiety disorder – intense anxiety or fear of being in social situations – is heritable: If you have a family member who has this disorder, you have a two to six times greater chance of having it as well.

Treatments for anxiety disorders include medication and psychotherapy. Medication does not cure but helps to manage the symptoms while the person works through the causes and effects of her particular disorder in psychotherapy. Specific psychotherapies are used for different types of anxiety disorders. It is also helpful to join therapy or support groups with those who have similar issues. As with depressive disorders, alternative remedies, such as, exercise, meditation, relaxation training, and deep breathing, have also been found to be beneficial in coping with anxiety disorders.

*Have you ever had any of the following symptoms? Please check any of the symptoms that apply to you. This checklist is not to be used to diagnose yourself or anyone else (only mental health professionals can assess accurately). Instead, use it to increase your understanding of anxiety disorders.*

☐ Excessive worry

☐ Intense fear

☐ Impaired concentration

☐ Restlessness

☐ Irritability

☐ Muscle tension

☐ Sleep disturbance

☐ Active avoidance of feared situation or object

☐ Physical features, e.g., accelerated heart rate, trembling, chest pain, numbness/tingling, shortness of breath

☐ Fear of losing control

*If you endorsed any of the above indicators, what caused you to experience those?*

_____

_____

_____

_____

*How did you manage the above symptoms?*

_____

_____

_____

_____

*Would you deal with them differently now? If yes, how?*

_____

_____

_____

_____

As with other reflective exercises throughout this curriculum, I have invited you to also reflect on your own experiences of depressive or anxiety features in order to become a more effective lay counselor. It is important to identify and accept signs within yourself (past/present) of these disorders, examine what has or has not helped you in your management of your symptoms, and increase your ability to relate to those who come to see you with these types of issues by recognizing that all of us are vulnerable to these problems if we do not intentionally work toward being healthy.

While lay counselors cannot provide psychotherapy or medication, you can still be tremendously helpful by using what you learned in the second session, *Building the Relational Context*, and encourage, support, motivate, and comfort those who are experiencing difficulties. You can also use the counseling tools learned in the third session: *prayer, deep breathing, biblical meditation, guided imagery, journaling,* and *cognitive restructuring*. As mentioned earlier, there is evidence that these practices increase physical and mental health in all of us.

# Session 7

## Addictions

"'I have the right to do anything,' you say — but not everything is beneficial. 'I have the right to do anything' — but I will not be mastered by anything" (1 Corinthians 6:12 NIV). We do have freedom in Jesus Christ in ways that those who lived in the Old Testament period did not: The latter were bound by laws that governed every area of their lives. For example, individuals were deemed "unclean" when they had skin infections, bodily discharges, ate certain foods, and touched dead bodies. They then had to undergo a purification process in order to approach others and God. We are set free from these types of laws to live in God's grace due to Christ's sacrifice. This does not mean, however, that we should do anything we want, because not everything is good for us, particularly those choices that can enslave us, such as, alcohol, drugs, food, sex, computer, pornography, and gambling, among others.

*Have you ever had an experience of continuing to engage in an activity even though it was causing problems (e.g., relational issues, health consequences, emotional toll, time management concerns, sleep disruptions) in your life? If yes, what was/is the behavior?*

_____

_____

_____

_____

_____

*What were/are the difficulties?*

_____

_____

_____

_____

*Were/are you able to stop this behavior? If yes, how? If no, why not?*

_____

_____

_____

_____

## What is Addiction?

In his book, *What's So Amazing About Grace?* Philip Yancey relays a story about a woman who sells herself and her young daughter to financially support her drug addiction.[1] This is an example of someone who has allowed her need for drugs to control her to such an extent that she is making unspeakable choices. While not every addict destroys his life in this way, everyone who suffers from an addiction makes negative life decisions due to:

- Dependence: preoccupation and craving of the object of their addiction, and

- Tolerance: needing more and more of the object of their addiction in order to experience the desired effect.

Those who are addicted find it very difficult to acknowledge how they are powerfully influenced by their cravings, which leads to loss of control and continued use, despite adverse consequences.

Addiction is a chronic disease that changes one's brain functioning by affecting the following systems: reward, pleasure, memory, motivation, and other related pathways in the brain. Addiction impairs one's thoughts by altering reality. The desire for the object of the addiction dominates one's thoughts, leading to skewed perceptions regarding what she needs, what makes her happy, what is beneficial, what is detrimental, etc. One's judgment is impaired.

It also has a damaging effect on behaviors. Addicts spend an inordinate amount of time and energy searching for, being engrossed in, and recovering from their addictive behaviors. Their actions cause problems at school, work, and with family members and peer groups. Their world becomes narrower, and all that really matters is the next time they can indulge in their addictions. They also struggle with impulse control and powerlessness to stop their addictive behaviors.

Addiction also affects people's emotions. While there is a positive impact ("high") initially when using the substances or engaging in addictive behaviors, over time, there is more anxiety, depression, and agitation, rather than pleasure, due to how one's brain adapts to the overstimulation of its reward/pleasure center. In addition, those who are addicted develop increased vulnerability to stress and its effects.

There are various types of addictions. Most well known and researched are alcohol and drug addictions. However, people can also become dependent on food, shopping, sex, pornography, gambling, exercise, computer and Internet use, among others, which leads to significant disruptions in normal daily functioning. In this session, we will study alcoholism, drug abuse, and Internet addiction, as these appear to be the most common addictions among church members from my experience in working with adolescents and adults in the church system.

## Alcoholism

Approximately 133 million Americans aged 12 or older report alcohol consumption.[2] Of this number, about 58 million people report binge drinking: for men, consuming 5 or more drinks, and for women, consuming 4 or more drinks – all within a 2-hour period. An estimated 18 million Americans suffer from alcoholism.[3] Alcoholism is a chronic disease that causes significant health, interpersonal, legal, financial, and/or occupational difficulties, and includes the following core characteristics:

- Craving: having a strong urge to drink

- Loss of control: having problems limiting how much one drinks

- Physical dependence: having withdrawal symptoms, e.g., trembling, sweating, and nausea, when one stops drinking

- Tolerance: having to drink more to get the same effect

Additional signs that one has alcoholism include lying and hiding about one's drinking, not remembering conversations or commitments that occurred while drinking, needing alcohol to relax, and having family and friends concerned about one's drinking. Some of these symptoms can be experienced without being diagnosed with alcoholism. However, if one consistently exhibits the above-mentioned characteristics and engages in binge drinking on a regular basis, one is likely to develop alcoholism.

Other risk factors include the following:

- Age of onset: The earlier one begins to drink alcohol, the more likely one is to develop alcoholism.

- Family history: Having a family member who has an alcohol addiction raises the probability of having similar problems with alcohol.

- Drinking regularly: The more one drinks on a consistent basis, the more likelihood that one will develop dependence and tolerance of alcohol.

- Mental disorders: If one has mental health issues, such as depression and anxiety, it increases one's risk for alcohol use disorders.

- Social factors: If one has close friends and/or significant other who drink on a regular basis, one is more likely to have problems with alcohol.

- Stressful life circumstances: The more stress one has, the more possibility that occasional alcohol consumption will become more frequent and consistent, prompting alcohol to be a primary coping tool, which then can result in alcohol addiction.

- Cultural customs: Cultural acceptance of consistent and excessive drinking leads to increased risk for alcoholism.

Alcohol affects one's thoughts, emotions, and behaviors. Excessive drinking leads to poor judgment, limited concentration, and faulty memory. It lowers inhibitions, leading to dangerous choices, such as, driving under the influence of alcohol, committing a violent crime, and having sex with someone one has just met. Long term drinking increases mental disorders, interpersonal difficulties, and work/school performance issues. Health consequences of alcoholism include increased risk of the following:[4]

- Bleeding in the digestive tract

- Brain cell damage

- Cancers of the esophagus, liver, colon, and other areas

- Erectile dysfunction

- Heart damage

- High blood pressure

- Liver disease

- Inflammation in the pancreas

Individuals who are suffering from alcoholism are clearly putting not only their health but also their lives at risk. If your client is struggling with alcohol addiction, it is imperative that you are honest about its effects on his life. You can provide support as he engages in various treatments, depending on his needs: detoxification programs; individual, family, and group psychotherapy; and residential inpatient treatments. You can also strongly recommend that he join support groups, such as, Alcoholics Anonymous (AA), which consists of recovering alcoholics who can provide comfort, encouragement, and strength to turn away from alcohol through its "12-step" program. It is also beneficial for his family to attend support groups, such as, Al-Anon, which helps them cope adaptively with having a family member with alcoholism.

If your client does not manifest symptoms of physical dependence and tolerance, but does exhibit other problematic behaviors related to alcohol, it is still important to have a candid and straightforward discussion about her use of alcohol. This includes what she drinks, how often she drinks, why she drinks, and how her drinking impacts various areas of her life. Illuminating the harmful effects of her drinking can help her to reduce or stop her problematic consumption of alcohol. It is also critical to replace alcohol use as a coping strategy with other positive tools, which you can teach (given what you learned in previous sessions). Individual, family, and group psychotherapy may be a necessary component of the recovery process.

Even when one succeeds in abstaining from alcohol, it is not uncommon to slip back into drinking at times. Thus, one of the most important elements in assisting someone in recovery is to facilitate sober family and peer environments to decrease potential triggers to drink. Continuous encouragement and support can also prevent relapse into alcohol use.

*Do you know of anyone who has problems with alcohol?*

☐ *Yes* ☐ *No*

*How have you tried to help this person?*

_____

_____

_____

*Were your efforts successful? Why or Why not?*

_____

_____

_____

*Is there anything you would do differently now? If yes, write down what you would change:*

_____

_____

_____

## Drug Addiction

In a 2011 national survey, approximately 23 million Americans aged 12 or older reported using illicit drugs, which include marijuana, cocaine, heroin, and prescription drugs not used for their intended purpose.[5] The highest drug use occurs in those in their late teens and twenties. Highest rate of increase in drug use is among those in their 50s. Marijuana is the most commonly used illegal substance at 7%. More than half of new illicit drug users begin with marijuana. Next most commonly used substance category is prescription pain relievers. About 2% of Americans abuse prescription drugs. About 54% of those abusing medications obtained them from a friend or a relative.

Similar to alcoholism, drug addiction is characterized by the presence of craving of the substance, loss of control over its use, physical dependence as manifested in withdrawal symptoms, tolerance effects, and continued use despite adverse consequences. Symptoms of drug abuse can also include neglecting one's responsibilities, feeling the need to take drugs to function every day, spending money on drugs even though one cannot afford it, taking risks to obtain drugs (e.g., stealing), and failing in one's attempts to reduce or stop using drugs.

Warning signs that someone may be abusing drugs include:[6]

- Physical: red eyes, deterioration in hygiene and grooming, tremors, slurred speech, diminished motor coordination

- Psychological: changes in personality, sudden mood swings, lack of energy or motivation, being fearful and paranoid

- Behavioral: decrease in performance at work/school, financial problems, secretive behaviors, abrupt changes in friends and activities

Different substances can cause divergent reactions. For example, marijuana use might result in red eyes, heightened perceptions, slowed reaction times, and paranoia. Abuse of stimulants, such as methamphetamine or Adderall (commonly used to treat attention-deficit/hyperactivity disorder) can lead to irritability, restlessness, sleep problems, weight loss, and increased heart rate. Misusing sedatives can cause memory problems, confusion, slowed breathing, drowsiness, and depression.

Many people use drugs recreationally. Some become addicted while others do not. Risk factors for developing drug addiction are similar to those of alcoholism. In addition to those listed in the alcoholism section, other risk factors include traumatic childhood experiences, parental neglect, and how one uses the drugs (e.g., injecting a drug increases the potential for addiction). When these circumstances, behaviors, and histories are present in an individual's life, one is more likely to develop a substance addiction. Thus, it is all the more critical that those who exhibit these risk factors do not start on the path of using substances.

Comparable to alcoholism, drug abuse and addiction can affect every area of one's life. It can lead to significant health problems;

increased risk for suicide; unconsciousness or even death when mixed with alcohol and/or when one takes multiple drugs at high doses; and legal, financial, social, and occupational difficulties.

Treatments for drug addiction, much like alcoholism, include inpatient residential treatment programs; individual, family, and group psychotherapies; and support groups. Depending on the severity of the drug problem, one may need to be in a detoxification program that safely helps one to stop using drugs by lessening the withdrawal effects so that one can more efficiently and effectively overcome his addiction. Like AA mentioned earlier, there is Narcotics Anonymous (NA) which consists of a group of recovering addicts who can provide support and guidance as one begins to take back his life and rebuild that which has been destroyed by drug use.

If you are working with someone who has problems with drugs, engage in an honest dialogue regarding your observations and offer your help as she goes through the recovery process. Persuade her to begin or continue the above-mentioned treatments. Talk with her about avoiding triggers. I worked with one patient who changed her phone number and deleted her drug dealer's phone number, so that she could not get in touch with him, and he could not contact her. In addition, she cut off her ties with her friends with whom she had engaged in drug use. You can also encourage your client to share her struggles with her family and friends, if she has not already done so, to receive further support and assistance. The more social support one has, the better the chance of recovery and the less the chance of relapse.

*Do you know of anyone who has problems with drug addiction?*

☐ *Yes* ☐ *No*

*How have you tried to help this person?*

_____

_____

_____

*Were your efforts successful? Why or Why not?*

_____

_____

_____

*Is there anything you would do differently now? If yes, write down what you would change:*

_____

_____

_____

## Internet Addiction

Pathological computer use has been a growing international concern in the recent decade. There is a news article even today reporting that the Japanese Ministry of Education believes that over 500,000 students (12-18 years old) are addicted to the Internet: It is asking the government to fund "fasting camps" to unplug children from their computers and other devices that keep them compulsively connected to a virtual world and not connected enough to their real world.[7] One of the first to establish such camps is S. Korea due to an estimated 30% of kids being at risk for Internet addiction with some dying of exhaustion after nonstop online gaming.[8] Because diagnostic criteria and assessment protocol have not been completely standardized for Internet addiction, there is a wide variance – 1.5%-8.2% – in reported prevalence rates in the U.S.[9]

Comparable to other addictions, Internet addiction can be characterized by the presence of preoccupation with and craving of digital media, loss of control over its use, withdrawal symptoms when one is digitally disconnected, need for more and more time online, and continued use despite negative consequences.[10] People who are addicted to the Internet will endorse the following questions:

☐ Are you frequently thinking about what you did previously on the Internet and anticipating the next online session?

☐ Have you failed in your attempts to reduce or stop your online activity?

☐ Do you feel irritable or depressed when you attempt to reduce or stop your Internet use?

☐ Do you get angry and defensive when you are interrupted?

☐ Have you hidden or lied about your Internet use?

☐ Do you lose track of time when you are on the Internet, and so stay online longer than you intended?

☐ Has your Internet use interfered with social or occupational functioning?

☐ Do you use the Internet as a way to escape from your problems?

Internet is a wonderful tool, and many use it to be more efficient and effective at work, to connect socially, and to access information and entertainment – with no harmful effects to one's daily life. However, more and more people are being absorbed into the virtual world of the Internet at the exclusion of participating in real life events and interactions. Those who have other mental health issues, such as, depression and anxiety, are more at risk for developing compulsive Internet use.

Additional risk factors that contribute to Internet addiction include suffering from other addictions, such as, alcohol and sex; social factors in which one's peers are using their computers in similar ways; experiencing stressful life events where they use the Internet to avoid dealing with their problems; and cultural contexts as demonstrated by higher prevalence rates in countries where there has been much more of an embracing of (and even taking pride in) using the Internet.

Much like other addictions, compulsive use of the Internet can negatively affect one's life. It can contribute to the development of various mental disorders, e.g., depression. It disrupts one's school and work functioning. It can also lead to conflicts in relationships as the addict spends more and more time on the Internet, and less and less time investing in relationships. One's physical health can be significantly impacted from making poor choices due to a consuming need to stay online, e.g., neglecting to eat and sleep regularly. In addition, one can develop back pain, headaches, neck strain, Carpel Tunnel syndrome, and strained vision.

It is crucial to intervene when you suspect that someone has an Internet addiction. Unlike alcohol and drug addictions, general abstinence is not the goal. Since the Internet provides necessary connections needed for functioning well in our culture and generation, treatment needs to target controlled use of the Internet. As mentioned above, some countries are utilizing "detox camps" to taper off problematic use. Individual, family, and group psychotherapy; support groups; and residential treatment centers are also helpful in treating Internet addiction. Medication for underlying disorders that may be contributing to inappropriate Internet use can also be an effective intervention option.

In terms of what you can do as lay counselors, you can work with the individual and his family toward healthy Internet use by encouraging the following:

- Increase awareness of one's problems by logging how often, when, how long one uses the Internet, etc.

- Set specific goals with regard to the above.

- Time the Internet use in between concrete, real-life events, e.g., between after school and the next scheduled activity where one is forced to log off.

- Change one's routine in terms of when one uses the Internet, e.g., if one usually uses it just before going to sleep, choose to log on in the morning instead.

- Find different, more effective ways to cope with stressors, e.g., going out with friends.

Perhaps you might start a support group in your community for kids who have developed an Internet addiction or for parents who are struggling with their kids' overuse of the Internet or for adults who are addicted to the Internet. Having a support group like this can increase the likelihood of changing one's problematic use of the Internet.

*Do you know of anyone who has problems with Internet addiction?*

☐ *Yes*  ☐ *No*

*How have you tried to help this person?*

_____

_____

_____

*Were your efforts successful? Why or Why not?*

_____

_____

_____

*Is there anything you would do differently now? If yes, write down what you would change:*

_____

_____

_____

In this session, we covered alcohol, drug, and Internet addictions. There are many other forms of addictions that interfere with living in the way that God intended. Most, if not all, share similarities in terms of risk factors, effects, and treatment modalities. Whatever form you encounter as a lay counselor, you can make a difference by encouraging and supporting your client's recovery process.

# Session 8

## Issues of Anger and Violence

There are multiple accounts of Jesus being angry in the Gospels – at sin, at the Pharisees, at the fruit-less fig tree, at the temple businessmen who used God's house, not for prayer but for their own gain, and at injustice. At its core, His anger is driven by "deep distress" over people's "stubborn hearts."[1] Jesus' anger is about feeling grieved due to people's hardened, uncompromising, legalistic attitudes and behaviors, which result in judgment and condemnation of others. He is saddened by the lack of compassion, love, and grace that people, especially the religious leaders of His day, exhibited. Ultimately, Jesus is angry because hearts and minds like these damage everyone, self included.

*What makes you angry?*

_____

_____

_____

## Anger

Anger is a healthy, normal, adaptive emotional state that all experience from time to time. It impacts us physically by increasing our energy hormones, heart rate, and blood pressure, so that we can mobilize our internal resources to protect ourselves from perceived danger. It aids in our survival, and moves us to care about and fight injustices. Thus, anger can be positive.

*Remember the last time you were angry. What happened?*

_____

_____

_____

_____

It is not anger itself that is at fault; it is how we express it that can potentially create problems. Some communicate anger appropriately by sharing their feelings of hurt and upset honestly, calmly, and directly – without condemning the other person or distorting what happened to justify one's anger.

Others suppress their feelings, including anger. Because it makes them feel uncomfortable, they deny, minimize, and distract themselves from their anger. This then causes the following:

- They turn anger inward, leading to mental and physical health issues, e.g., depressive disorders and hypertension.

- They express anger in passive-aggressive ways, e.g., they are mad at someone for not paying back a loan, but instead of confronting the person, they start gossiping about this person to others.

- They displace their anger from one person or event to another, e.g., they are angry at their spouse for not supporting them during a conflict with their in-laws, but instead of letting their spouse know and working through this issue together, they say nothing to the spouse, but shout at their kids.

- They become more critical and hostile in general, constantly finding fault with everyone and everything.

Many express anger by lashing out at others, thereby causing emotional, mental, relational, and/or physical harm. They may lose their temper and curse, throw objects around or at the person they are angry with, become sullen and uncommunicative, and/or physically injure the person they think caused them to be upset. They tend to lose their tempers easily, blame others for their problems, have limited tolerance for being thwarted from their expectations, and be inflexible about how things should be.

*How do you usually express your anger?*

_____

_____

_____

*Where did you learn to express it this way?*

_____

_____

_____

_____

*Describe anything you would like to change:*

_____

_____

_____

## Violence

How one commonly expresses one's anger depends on genetic predisposition and environmental factors. Some appear to be born more irritable, easily angered, and moody. Many learn how to communicate their feelings, including anger, by observing how their family members handle them. Individuals who grow up in disruptive, chaotic, and violent homes tend to be easily provoked into expressing anger inappropriately. Culture also plays a role: If lashing out in anger is tolerated in one's community, one is more likely to express his anger in this way. In addition, when people are exposed to characters reacting aggressively in the media or in the online world, they become desensitized and more accepting of violence as a way to express anger.

Being perpetually violent with one's anger leads to various difficulties. It can lead to physical health problems, such as, heart disease, compromised immune system, and diabetes. It also causes mental health issues, such as, decreased concentration, distorted perceptions of events and interactions, and lack of energy to function well in all areas of life. Furthermore, it negatively impacts one's relationships in the workplace, church, social gatherings, and home.

Violence that occurs in the home is a type of abuse, and is labeled "domestic violence." Its chief purpose is to control and dominate family members through verbal and physical intimidation. Violence can be directed at one's spouse, children, and elderly relatives. It includes physical injuries, sexual abuse, threats of violence, and psychological abuse. While there are men who are victims of domestic violence, most often it is a crime that is committed by men against children and women.[2] Research shows that 25% of women will experience violence in their lifetime. Each year, 33% of women who are victims of homicide are killed by their former or current partners. More than three million children witness domestic violence annually, and among these, 30-60% suffer abuse as well.[3]

Those who abuse their partners tend to be extremely jealous of anyone and anything that takes time, attention, and resources away from them. They are unquestionably the head of their household whose rules are to be obeyed without question; otherwise, there are severe consequences. They frequently criticize, shame, and treat their partners badly in front of others. They intimidate through making threatening remarks and/or actions against children, throwing objects, destroying what one values, and hurting pets, among other terrorizing behaviors. It is also common for the abusers to deny or minimize the harm they inflicted as well as to blame their words and actions on the victims (e.g., "If you hadn't made me so angry…")

What victims of domestic violence experience:

- Being afraid of one's partner

- "Walking on eggshells"

- Avoiding certain issues for fear of angering one's partner

- Checking in constantly with one's partner

- Recurrent injuries that seem suspicious

- Frequent absences from work, school, and/or social functions

- Limited access to money, phone, and/or car

- Restriction of people with whom one can talk and/or meet

- Feeling depressed, anxious, helpless, and/or numb

Domestic violence follows a predictable pattern beginning with a violent behavior for some transgressions – real or imagined; then excuses and apologies for that behavior by the abuser; then a normal period where everything seems fine and the victim begins to hope that life will be better; then buildup of tension and anger in the perpetrator; and then violence occurs again. The abuser's contrition and caring attitudes and behaviors in between abusive episodes make it difficult for victims to leave.

As a lay counselor, if you are meeting with someone you suspect to be suffering from domestic violence and abuse, refer her to mental health professionals, local shelters for women and children, support groups, and National Domestic Violence Hotline (1-800-799-7233). There are legal and ethical concerns surrounding issues of domestic violence, which will be covered in a future session. Do not blame, pressure, minimize, or give advice about what she should do. Instead, alongside the professionals who are working with her, you can:

- Listen to her thoughts, feelings, and stories, without judgment or condemnation.

- Empathize with what she has been experiencing.

- Offer assistance, e.g., accompany her to a shelter.

- Provide support.

One of the most helpful messages that she can receive from you is that she is not alone in this anymore – that you and other people are there to help her as needed.

If you discover that the person you are working with fits the above description of an abuser, refer him to individual psycho-therapy, treatment programs for batterers, and pastoral counseling. If he participates in these interventions, accepts responsibility for what he has done, and exhibits willingness to do whatever is needed to change the dynamics in the family, then you can meet with him to support the work he is doing with the professionals.

## Anger Management

The first task in managing one's anger is to prevent escalation. It is important to pay attention to warning signs that one's irritation is building into rage:

- Physiological:

  - Faster heart rate

  - Tensing one's shoulders, jaw or hands

  - Needing to pace

- Emotional:

  - Feeling justified in one's anger

  - Feeling disregarded

  - Feeling misunderstood

- Cognitive:

  - Blaming others

  - Overgeneralizing, e.g., "You always/never…"

  - "Shoulds" and "musts," e.g., when reality does not fit with one's idea of what should/must happen, one becomes angry

Be aware of the above signs, and take steps to reduce these symptoms so that one's anger does not continue unchecked into fury.

In addition to identifying and managing one's warning signs of escalating anger, it is also important to understand one's triggers. What usually leads to feeling irritated, outraged, and infuriated? Here is a common scenario that occurs in many homes: Mom becomes furious at her child when she has to ask him – for the fifth time – to get his homework done before he plays on the computer. This is a script that this mom-child pair experiences almost on a daily basis. Thus, it is highly predictable that the next time mom has to ask repetitively for her child to do this, she will get angry when he does not comply.

When she realizes that this is a repetitive pattern, she could choose to think, feel, and behave differently, which will cause a different outcome. For example, she might re-think the idea that her child has to finish all of his homework before he can play: Maybe it will not be so terrible to have him play a limited amount of time after school before he begins his homework. After all, he has been working all day at school, and may need a break, much like adults. Also, instead of feeling totally disrespected when he does not obey, she might consider that it is not about being dismissive of her, but about him: his need to have a say in what he wants to do, his desire to have fun, his anxiety about his homework which leads to procrastination, etc. If she can relate to these possibilities, it will mitigate her anger. Finally, she might establish some rules, such as, he needs to listen when she asks the first time, otherwise, there will be consequences. This way, she is not continually getting more and more annoyed as he continues to seemingly disregard her requests. By recognizing what precipitates one's angry reactions, it is possible to predict and prepare for theses types of situations so that one can handle them more effectively.

It is also helpful to understand any underlying issues that fuel one's anger. Perhaps what one is really feeling is fear, and one expresses this as anger, due to ingrained messages that being afraid is unacceptable. This is particularly true for men in certain cultures. Thus, instead of expressing anxiety over a situation, they manifest hostility and fury. I have had many male patients for whom anger is a mask for fearfulness and shame. Or perhaps one believes that one is always right, and when someone disagrees with one's perspectives, it can be enraging. Usually, an individual like this tends to be very controlling, and it feels threatening to his fragile sense of self to listen to someone with different viewpoints. Or perhaps one is constantly yelling at one's child, when really the person one is mad at, is one's spouse. It is "safer" to be angry with someone who is more vulnerable and who cannot retaliate in ways that one fears. When the underlying issues are acknowledged and understood, the anger that is expressed can be modified to better fit the situations.

*Imagine that you are meeting with an angry young man. Delineate how you would approach him to help him deal with his anger:*

_____

_____

_____

_____

_____

As lay counselors, you can work with kids and adults on identifying signs of escalation from irritation to rage, precipitating factors to expressions of anger, and underlying issues that contribute to feelings of frustration. You can also coach them through effectively managing their anger by teaching some of the tools studied earlier, such as, *deep breathing, meditation, journaling,* and *cognitive restructuring.* In addition, you can encourage them to exercise, let out some of the aggression on a heavy bag, and take some time to cool down (e.g., count to 20 and put oneself in timeout) before confronting the situation and/or the person. When anger is managed effectively, it can be used to change interactions and events in positive ways.

# Session 9

## Childhood Mental Disorders

When I read the Gospel accounts, it seems to me that Jesus has a special heart for those who are vulnerable and oppressed, including children. Jesus made time for them and encouraged adults to be like them – transparent, sensitive, curious, and teachable. It is important to protect and nurture these characteristics so that children feel free and empowered to develop their God-given talents and passions. When parents brought their children to Jesus, His disciples rebuked them. They did not think children were important enough to be brought to Jesus' attention or to need His care.[1] When Jesus saw this, He reprimanded his disciples: It is clear that children are of great value to Jesus. For many cultures and generations, children have been viewed as possessions and extensions of their parents with no voice of their own, and perhaps this contributes to some of the childhood mental disorders observed today.

### Statistics

It is estimated that about 20% of children (3-17 years old) in the U.S. suffer from debilitating mental disorders.[2] Many of the childhood mental disorders continue through adulthood. In fact, among life-long sufferers of mental illnesses, approximately 50% of them begin to manifest symptoms when they are 14 years old.[3] Thus, if we are able to prevent or intervene early in one's development of mental disorders, one is less likely to be at risk for being impaired as an adult.

The most prevalent disorders in children are those related to attention-deficit/ hyperactivity (ADHD), conduct, and anxiety. Certain conditions, such as ADHD, conduct disorder, and autism spectrum disorder, are more common in boys, while other difficulties, such as depression and anxiety, are more likely to occur in girls. The following are some of the other childhood mental illness categories: intellectual disabilities, communication disorders, motor disorders, obsessive-compulsive disorders, trauma- and stress- related disorders, sleep-wake disorders, eating disorders, and substance-related and addictive disorders.

## Causes of Mental Disorders in Children

Similar to adults, mental disorders in children are most often caused by a combination of biological and environmental factors. If a parent of a child has a mental disorder, his child will have a predisposition to manifesting these disorders. In addition, if a child experiences trauma, such as, sexual abuse, she will be more likely to develop certain symptoms. If a child undergoes stressful life events, e.g., being bullied, this may also contribute to the onset of psychological problems in the child. Brain injuries, malnutrition, substance use, and certain temperament may also play a role in causing mental health issues to emerge.

## General Signs of Distress

While each disorder within various classifications has specific criteria that need to be met for a child to be diagnosed, there are general signs that may indicate mental health problems:

- Increased social isolation

- Loss of interest in previously enjoyable activities

- Frequent physical complaints

- Sleep and eating disturbances

- Angry outbursts

- Aggressive behaviors

- Excessive worry

- Sense of sadness and hopelessness

- Signs of self-destructive behaviors, e.g., head-banging

- Regressing to earlier developmental stages, e.g., not wanting to be separated from parents

- Problems across various areas, e.g., academics, friendships, at home, etc.

*As a child, did you experience any of the above markers of distress? If yes, explain.*

_____

_____

_____

_____

_____

Many children experience a normal range of distress as a result of various life circumstances. For example, if a child loses a parent, she will experience many of the symptoms listed above for a period of time, and they would be normal reactions to her grief. However, children who are diagnosed with a mental disorder will manifest a specified number of symptoms, which represent a persistent pattern of behavior, thinking, and/or feeling that have been occurring for a stipulated length of time. These traits are disruptive enough to cause academic, social, and occupational impairments.

## ADHD

ADHD is characterized by significant problems in attention, impulsivity, and hyperactivity. This is one of the most common childhood mental disorders, with 7% of children being diagnosed with it in any given year.[4] While it is one of the disorders that can continue through adolescence and into adulthood, symptoms need to have been present in childhood, usually before age 7, in order to be diagnosed. It is observed more frequently in boys than girls (ratio of 2:1). There are three types of ADHD:[5]

- Predominantly inattentive presentation: fails to pay attention to details, difficulty sustaining attention, does not follow through on instructions, loses things, easily distracted

- Predominantly hyperactive/impulsive presentation: fidgets constantly, cannot stay seated, talks excessively, runs about inappropriately, interrupts or intrudes on others

- Combined presentation: both of the above symptoms exist

Particular ADHD symptoms can be more strongly manifested at different developmental stages: Hyperactivity may be more noticeable in earlier years, while inattentiveness and impulsivity may be more pronounced in later years.

There are many factors correlated with increased risk for ADHD: having a family member who is diagnosed with ADHD, very low birth weight, exposure to alcohol and nicotine in utero, history of child abuse, exposure to neurotoxins, infections, and nutritional deficiencies. Thus, genetic, physiological, and environmental variables contribute to the onset of ADHD.

Children who are diagnosed with ADHD frequently perform poorly in school, have interpersonal conflicts with family and friends, and struggle with self-esteem issues. They are also more likely to develop other disorders, including learning disabilities, anxiety, depression, and substance abuse.

Treatments for ADHD include medications, such as, Adderall and Concerta, used to control the symptoms of hyperactivity, impulsivity, and inattentiveness. In addition, individual and family psychotherapy, social skills training groups, and behavioral management coaching have also been found to be helpful in dealing with this disorder more effectively.

As lay counselors, if you suspect that you are meeting with a family where ADHD appears to be an issue, refer the family to a mental health professional to be properly evaluated and treated. You can provide prayer, encouragement, and positive reinforcement of the changes being established in the family through various therapies. You can also initiate and facilitate a support group for parents with children suffering from ADHD.

*As far as you know, did you or any family member suffer from ADHD as a child? If yes, explain:*

_____

_____

_____

_____

*How do you think your answer will affect your work as a lay counselor?*

_____

_____

_____

_____

## Conduct Disorder

Many children and adolescents experience normal amounts of behavioral issues. They may occasionally lie, cheat, act impulsively, be truant, or be insolent. However, when these behaviors become a constant source of trouble (especially between youth and authority figures) and are disruptive to academic, social, and occupational functioning, then they may be suffering from a conduct disorder. This is characterized by a pervasive pattern of behavior in which societal rules and rights of others are disregarded. Conduct disorder occurs in approximately 4% of children and adolescents, not only in the U.S., but also in other countries.[5] Prevalence rates increase from childhood to adolescence, and more boys than girls are diagnosed with this condition. There are four clusters of symptoms:

- Aggression to people and animals, e.g., bullies, initiates fights, is physically cruel to animals and people

- Destruction of property, e.g., fire setting

- Deceitfulness or theft, e.g., breaking into other peoples' homes, lying to get what he wants, stealing

- Serious violation of rules, e.g., stays out late despite parental objections, runs away from home, truant from school

Conduct disorder can be classified as mild (minimum criteria for the diagnosis is met with relatively minor harm to others), moderate (more symptoms are endorsed with some harm to others), or severe (more than enough to make the diagnosis with significant harm to others). A small segment of those diagnosed with a conduct disorder are also designated with the label, "with limited prosocial emotions," meaning that they lack remorse or guilt for their wrongdoing, lack empathy, are unconcerned about poor performance in various areas, and appear insincere and shallow in their affect.

Many variables contribute to the occurrence of a conduct disorder. As with many mental disorders, if one has a family member who is diagnosed with this condition, one is more likely to develop it. In addition, if one's family member is diagnosed with other mental disorders, such as, alcoholism, bipolar disorders, or ADHD, one is more at risk for developing a conduct disorder. It has also been consistently noted that those who are diagnosed with this condition have (a) slower resting heart rate in comparison to other groups of people and (b) different brain structure and functioning in areas regulating their emotions. Risk factors for conduct disorder also include being temperamental as an infant and having a lower-than-average intelligence. Environmental variables that increase one's chance of developing a conduct disorder are as follows: child abuse, lack of parental supervision, family history of substance abuse, delinquent peer group, living in high-crime neighborhoods, and traumatic life experiences.

Kids who fit this diagnostic category tend to have frequent school suspensions, legal problems, and physical injuries from engaging in dangerous behaviors. They are also more likely to have accidents, sexually transmitted diseases, and unplanned pregnancies. In addition, they may have coexisting mental disorders, such as, anxiety, depression, and ADHD.

Intervention for those with conduct disorder typically involves individual psychotherapy to increase anger management, impulse control, moral reasoning, and problem solving skills. Family therapy is also recommended to establish effective communication and healthy interactions among family members. Additionally, in-home behavioral management therapy can be beneficial in reducing disruptive behaviors. This is usually an intensive, short-term service provided by a team of clinicians who collaborates with family members, school staff, and other mental health providers.

As lay counselors, you can help the youth and/or the family strengthen new attitudes, choices, and behaviors that they are establishing with their mental health professionals. In addition, here again, you can form and lead a group for parents to provide support, encouragement, and accountability, all of which can be valuable in contributing to positive changes.

*As far as you know, did you or any family member suffer from conduct disorder as a child? If yes, explain:*

_____

_____

_____

_____

*How do you think your answer will affect your work as a lay counselor?*

_____

_____

_____

## Anxiety Disorders

All children experience anxiety from time to time. It is develop-
mentally appropriate for infants to have short-term anxiety around
strangers; toddlers to fear the dark and monsters; children to worry
about natural disasters; and teenagers to be nervous about taking
tests, performing in public, and being liked. However, not every
child or adolescent experiences the full range of symptoms required
for an anxiety disorder diagnosis nor are their fears and worries
considered irrational and excessive to the point where they structure their lives to avoid exposure to these feared circumstances.

Approximately 8% of adolescents experience an anxiety disorder
in any given year.[6] Lifetime prevalence rate of teen anxiety disorders can rise as high as 25%. Symptoms may begin as early as age
6. Girls are more likely than boys to be diagnosed with anxiety disorders.

Types of anxiety disorders that are observed in childhood include:[5]

- Separation anxiety disorder: overwhelming fear of being separated from their caregivers and their homes

- Specific phobia: fear of specific object or situation, e.g., fear of
  heights, dogs, riding in elevators

- Social anxiety disorder: intense apprehension in social situations or speaking in front of others

- Obsessive-compulsive disorder: preoccupation with disturbing thoughts and repetitive rituals to alleviate them

- Generalized anxiety disorder: chronic, excessive worry about
  everything

- Panic disorder: unexpected, intense anxiety characterized by
  physical symptoms, e.g., shortness of breath, increased heart
  rate, numbness or tingling

- Posttraumatic stress disorder: anxiety manifested in symptoms, e.g., nightmares and flashbacks, resulting from an exposure to a trauma

Most of these disorders can also be found in adults. Each of these disorders has specific criteria that need to be met for an individual to be diagnosed. Usually, the symptoms have to exist for six months or more and cause significant distress in important areas of one's life. Depending on the type of the anxiety disorder, one's functioning can be mildly impaired to severely disabled. For example, if one has a specific phobia to needles, this will not affect daily functioning in the way that a social anxiety disorder might. The latter is associated with increased rates of school dropout, and decreased quality of life, particularly as a result of lack of social engagement and support.

Combination of biological and environmental factors contributes to an emergence of an anxiety disorder. Those who have family members who suffer from some form of anxiety disorder are at greater risk for developing an anxiety disorder. Brain imaging studies of youths diagnosed with anxiety disorders demonstrate atypical functioning in certain brain structures that regulate emotions, particularly fear.[7] Children who are shy and cautious are more likely to eventually manifest an anxiety disorder. In addition, those children and adolescents who have experienced abuse, certain parenting practices (e.g., controlling and overprotective), and significant stressors in their lives, are predisposed to incidences of anxiety disorders.

Individual psychotherapy is the primary method of treatment to reduce or eliminate symptoms. Medications sometimes are utilized, depending on the type and severity of the anxiety disorders. They do not cure these disorders, just control the symptoms while the work is being done in psychotherapy. As with other medications, those used for these conditions have risks associated with them.

As lay counselors, if you are meeting with someone who is suffering from anxiety, provide guidance and encouragement as learned in the sessions on *Building the Relational Context* and *Counseling Tools*. You can facilitate an anxiety management group for kids not only to provide a safe place for youths to come together with other children or teenagers to share their struggles and support each other, but also to teach skills, such as *deep breathing* and *guided imagery*, which are helpful in reducing anxiety. You can also lead a support group for parents whose kids are suffering with an anxiety disorder. As always, by providing additional help to enhance the work they are doing with mental health providers, their treatment may be more effective.

*As far as you know, did you or any family member suffer from any anxiety disorders? If yes, explain:*

_____

_____

_____

_____

*How do you think your answer will affect your work as a lay counselor?*

_____

_____

_____

_____

Throughout this session, I asked you to share whether you or anyone in your family has suffered from various disorders. In order to help others acknowledge, understand, and accept their disorders, it is essential to acknowledge, understand, and accept symptoms in yourself and/or in your family members.

In addition, it is important to know how your personal experiences influence your lay counseling work: what and how you hear what your client is sharing, and how you respond to them. There are positive and negative implications of knowing these types of mental health difficulties personally. For example, the benefit of having been diagnosed with ADHD and working with families where this is an issue is that you might have greater empathy for them; however, the drawback might be that you might minimize their issues if your own symptoms abated over the years (e.g., "I had ADHD as a child, but I'm doing just fine now even without treatment, and so, yours will be fine too eventually"). If you have had a family member who has been diagnosed with conduct disorder, and this caused significant distress in the family, this may also color your perceptions and responses. Given your personal experience, you may have a better understanding of what family members go through, but you also might react more negatively than the situation warrants, as a result of being more sensitive to this issue. Thus, it is crucial to be aware of yourself and how you filter information, so that you can more clearly hear those who come to you for help.

# Session 10

## Personality Disorders

Have you ever thought about Jesus' personality? His character is one that draws people – that invites people to engage with Him. We can observe His personality in how He relates to others in the Gospel narratives. He is assertive in expressing Himself, compassionate in reaching out to those who are wounded, methodical in His ministry, secure in His calling, and open to challenging old traditions, among other traits.

Many of us have had experiences with people who are difficult to love. We have encountered individuals whom everyone finds challenging. We might even feel this way about ourselves. Have you had difficulty getting along with others on a consistent basis? This session will focus on how one's personality can interfere with having a healthy emotional, social, and spiritual life.

### What is Personality?

It is a distinctive set of traits that makes us who we are. It refers to a relatively consistent pattern of thoughts, feelings, and behaviors that influences our experiences of others and ourselves. Among the various ways of exploring and understanding personality, the *Five-Factor Model* offers one of the most researched and validated frameworks.[1] It provides a general personality structure across five dimensions:

| Personality Factor | Characteristics of Individuals High in Factor | Characteristics of Individuals Low in Factor |
| --- | --- | --- |
| Extraversion | Active<br>Talkative<br>Assertive<br>Energetic | Passive<br>Quiet<br>Solitary<br>Reserved |
| Agreeableness | Cooperative<br>Friendly<br>Trusting<br>Compassionate | Hostile<br>Selfish<br>Untrusting<br>Unkind |
| Conscientiousness | Organized<br>Methodical<br>Reliable<br>Efficient | Careless<br>Negligent<br>Easily Distracted<br>Mellow |
| Neuroticism | Nervous<br>Moody<br>Insecure<br>Sensitive | Even-tempered<br>Stable<br>Secure<br>Confident |
| Openness to Experience | Imaginative<br>Curious<br>Creative<br>Insightful | Practical<br>Traditional<br>Down-to-earth<br>Cautious |

*I have listed the factors and their opposites below. Where do you fall in the above dimensions? Please mark with an "x."*

Extraverted ——————————————————————— Introverted

Agreeable ——————————————————————— Antagonistic

Conscientious ——————————————————————— Impulsive

Neurotic ——————————————————————— Emotionally Stable

Open ——————————————— Closed to New Experiences

*How do you feel about your personality?*

_____

_____

_____

_____

Personality is affected by both biological and environmental factors, such as, genetics, brain structure, parenting practices, peer influences, and trauma. Depending on the interplay of these variables, one can develop a personality disorder.

### What is a Personality Disorder?

It is a type of mental disorder in which a person's ingrained, chronic thoughts, feelings, and behaviors are different from the norm. It is manifested in an enduring pattern of rigid and unhealthy ways of thinking, affectivity, and relating to people and situations, which can cause significant difficulties across important areas of functioning. Features of a personality disorder need to be identified by early adulthood. People suffering from personality disorders may feel that the manner in which they are functioning are natural and normal. However, their inner experiences and external actions contrast significantly with societal and cultural standards.

Risk factors for developing personality disorders include the following:[2]

- Genetic predisposition or vulnerability, e.g., there is some evidence that those who have relatives with schizophrenia are more likely to exhibit cluster A personality disorders (described below)

- Neurological abnormalities, e.g., in brain structures that regulate emotion, impulsivity, and aggression

- Childhood trauma, e.g., verbal, physical, or sexual abuse

- High reactivity or overly sensitive temperament

Having a significant, positive relationship with a family member, teacher, or friend can buffer the effects of the above risk factors. In other words, having a supportive individual or group can decrease the likelihood of developing personality disorders.

In order to be diagnosed with a personality disorder, an individual must fit certain criteria as delineated in DSM-5.[3] There are three categories (based on similar characteristics) of personality disorders:

- Cluster A: Characterized by odd, eccentric cognitions and behaviors

- Cluster B: Characterized by dramatic, overly emotional cognitions and behaviors

- Cluster C: Characterized by anxious, fearful cognitions and behaviors

Personality disorders are usually observable by adolescence and continue through adulthood. It is estimated that approximately 15% of U.S. adults suffer from at least one personality disorder.[2] Prevalence rates for each of the Clusters are as follows: 6% for Cluster A, 2% for Cluster B, and 9% for Cluster C.

Cluster A includes paranoid, schizoid, and schizotypal personality disorders. Those suffering from paranoid personality disorder exhibit pervasive mistrust and suspicion of others. They are preoccupied with believing that others are trying to harm them. They tend to perceive hidden negative meanings to innocuous comments, react defensively, and bear grudges.

Those who are diagnosed with schizoid personality disorder manifest a pattern of detachment from social relationships and a restricted range of expression of emotions in interpersonal settings. They appear emotionally cold, solitary, and indifferent to others' opinions. They do not desire close relationships or take pleasure in activities with others.

Those who are impaired due to schizotypal personality disorder are characterized by intense anxiety in social situations and perceptual distortions. They tend to hold odd, unconventional beliefs, such as, existence of telepathy and clairvoyance. They speak in eccentric ways and appear peculiar to others. Their social relationships, which are virtually nonexistent, are filtered through a paranoid lens.

Cluster B includes antisocial, borderline, narcissistic, and histrionic personality disorders. Those diagnosed with antisocial personality disorder are characterized by a pervasive pattern of disregard for and violation of the rights of others, which have been occurring since age 15. These individuals display a callous unconcern for the feelings of others and lack empathy. They consistently flout social conventions and rules, and thus, find themselves in trouble with the law often. They have very low frustration tolerance and a low threshold for violence. They lack guilt and tend to blame others or situations for their misbehaviors.

Those suffering from borderline personality disorder have unstable relationships, self-image, and moods. They exhibit a pattern of intense interpersonal relationships that alternate between extremes of positive and negative judgments. They are noticeably impulsive in ways that are potentially self-damaging, e.g., they can be promiscuous, drive recklessly, and abuse substances. They tend to make recurrent suicidal threats, gestures, and attempts. They also engage in self-mutilating behaviors, such as cutting and burning. They are ruled by fear of abandonment and chronic feelings of emptiness. They tend to have difficulty controlling their anger and react in inappropriate rage to perceived hurts.

Narcissistic personality disorder is characterized by need for admiration, lack of empathy, and grandiosity. Those who are diagnosed with this disorder tend to have an exaggerated sense of self-importance, and believe that they are "special" and should associate with other people of high importance. They are preoccupied with fantasies of unlimited success, power, brilliance, or beauty. They have an unreasonable expectation of how well they should be treated. They demonstrate a marked lack of empathy and can easily exploit others for their own gain.

Those who are impaired due to histrionic personality disorder tend to display excessive emotionality and attention seeking behaviors. They express themselves in shallow and rapidly changing emotions and words. They interact with others in provocative and sexually inappropriate ways. They consistently draw attention to themselves via their physical appearances. They are easily influenced by others and consider their relationships to be more intimate than they actually are.

Cluster C includes avoidant, dependent, and obsessive-compulsive personality disorders. Avoidant personality disorder is marked by a pattern of social avoidance, feelings of inadequacy, and sensitivity to judgment. Those who fall into this classification have a persistent feeling of apprehension about being in interpersonal situations due to feeling socially inept, personally unappealing, or inferior. They are extremely concerned with being rejected or criticized in social settings. Thus, they avoid social activities, and their lives are restricted as a result.

Those who are diagnosed with dependent personality disorder tend to rely too much on others to meet their physical and emotional needs. They cannot make any decisions without an excessive amount of advice and reassurance from others. They have trouble disagreeing with others for fear of losing their support. They will go to extreme lengths to ensure that they have others' nurturance, support, and help. They have intense fears about being alone and are insecure about taking care of themselves. They need others to be responsible for them.

Those who suffer from obsessive-compulsive personality disorder (OCPD) tend to be preoccupied with perfectionism, control, and orderliness. They can be quite rigid, closed minded, pedantic, and inefficient. The major point of a task or activity is lost amidst details, rules, and schedules. Their perfectionism can cost them the completion of a job. They tend to be overly conscientious about morality and ethics. They cannot delegate work to others, because they are afraid that the task will not get done exactly as they wish.

*As you consider the various personality disorders, is there one that particularly stands out for you? If yes, please explain.*

_____

_____

_____

_____

We might be more interested in a particular disorder, because we see ourselves or loved ones depicted in it. It is important to remember that we exist on a normal to abnormal continuum, and thus, it is common to identify certain characteristics in ourselves with what we read. For example, college education is correlated with OCPD.[4] Thus, those of us who are college educated may display some of the features of OCPD, but this does not mean that we have this disorder. In addition, depending on the dynamics of our relationships with our family members, we may filter certain attributes to fit with our perceptions of a particular family member. That is, if you have struggled with a sibling who has been quite dependent on your parents, you might wonder whether he has a dependent personality disorder. If you suspect yourself or someone else of having a personality disorder, it is critical to be assessed and treated by a mental health professional.

If personality disorders are left untreated, they will cause significant difficulties in people's lives. They may also worsen over time without treatment. Psychotherapy is the primary form of treatment. Through individual, couples, and/or family counseling, one can work through the symptoms and underlying issues in order to experience a healthier sense of self as well as of others. Specific therapies effective for treating personality disorders are as follows:

- Cognitive Behavioral Therapy (CBT) focuses on resolving symptoms that interfere with healthy functioning. These therapies help to identify and change distorted, negative thoughts and behaviors that contribute to the symptoms of personality disorders.

- Dialectical Behavior Therapy (DBT) concentrates on teaching behavioral skills to help people tolerate stress, regulate emotions, and improve relationships with others.

- Psychodynamic Therapy helps individuals to increase awareness of unconscious thoughts and behaviors, develop new insights into one's motivations, and resolve conflicts – internal and external – to live a more integrated, healthier life.

- Psycho-education seeks to inform those suffering as well as their loved ones to understand what personality disorders are and how to cope adaptively with various symptoms.

In addition to psychotherapy, medications are also an option. There are no medications specifically designed for personality disorders. However, there are several types of psychotropic medications that may be helpful in supporting the work in psychotherapy by stabilizing other conditions. For example, antidepressants can be used if one suffers from depressed mood, impulsivity, and/or anger. Anti-anxiety medications can be used if one suffers from anxiety, agitation, and/or insomnia. Antipsychotic medications can be used if one suffers from hallucinations, delusions, and/or poor reality contact. All of these will serve to reduce disorders that interfere with healthy functioning while the client focuses on their personality issues. In severe cases of personality disorders (e.g., someone with a borderline personality disorder who has attempted multiple suicides), psychiatric hospitalization may be needed, which can include 24-hour inpatient care for a designated time frame, partial/day care, or residential treatment.

As lay counselors, you can help identify troubling thoughts, feelings, and behaviors – especially those that impair relationships in the home, workplace, and/or church – and express your concerns to your client. It is important not to enable those suffering from personality disorders to continue their disturbing behaviors. Do not make excuses for their hurtful choices. Do not minimize or deny how they are affecting others. What this means is that you need to be honest, straightforward, and firm about your observations.

This is consistent with Matthew 18:15 where Jesus states, "If your brother or sister sins, go and point out their fault, just between the two of you…" Having a personality disorder is not a sin: It is an illness. However, as a result of having this disorder, one can sin by being hateful to themselves and others. It is important to speak truth in love in order to facilitate healing and recovery in the person, her family, and the larger family that is the church community. Personality disorders are hard to tolerate, especially for those who have to live with the people who have them. By providing support, encouragement, and prayer to your client and his family, you are doing your part in promoting mental health.

# Session 11

## Self-Evaluation and Referrals

You have now spent the past 10 weeks training to be a part of the lay counseling ministry in your church. It is my hope that you have a clear understanding of what this ministry entails, various mental health issues that may surface among your church members, and how to help those suffering from emotional, mental, and relational distress. What do you think about this ministry and your place in it? How do you feel about being part of this ministry? Is lay counseling ministry a good fit for you?

### Self-Evaluation

In the first session of this training series, I highlighted the importance of certain characteristics in those who are called to be lay counselors. The following is a more comprehensive list of traits that are desirable in lay counselors:

- A stable, personal relationship with God

- Passion for helping others:
  - To heal mentally, emotionally, and relationally
  - To change and grow positively

- Spiritual gifts:

- Knowledge

- Wisdom

- Discernment

- Encouragement

- Mercy

- Personal characteristics:

  - Self-Awareness

  - Empathy

  - Warmth

  - Patience

  - Openness to hearing divergent viewpoints

  - Respect for boundaries

  - Genuine interest in people

  - High ethical standards (especially as it pertains to confidentiality)

*Reflect on the above, and describe how you fit the qualities of someone who can be an effective lay counselor:*

_____

_____

_____

_____

_____

_____

*Check with others in your lay counseling ministry training group and your community to verify your perceptions. Do they agree or disagree with your evaluation of yourself? Please explain:*

_____

_____

_____

_____

Being a good counselor does not mean that you have all the characteristics listed above. The first two – spiritual maturity, and passion for helping others heal and grow – are prerequisites for being part of the lay counseling ministry. However, if you have some of the talents (i.e., spiritual gifts and personal characteristics) enumerated, then you have the potential to be an effective counselor.

If you decide at this point that you will not pursue being part of the lay counseling ministry, you can still use what you learned in this training to be a more effective leader, particularly when you face church members who suffer from mental, emotional, and relational issues. Regardless of your decision to be a lay counselor, it is important to know the referral process as you serve the church in various capacities.

## Referrals

While there is much that you can do as lay counselors and leaders in the church community, there are certain individuals, couples, families, and situations that warrant professional care. It is critical to be aware of when, how, and to whom you should refer, in order to increase the likelihood that everyone is receiving the help they need.

## When Do I Refer?

In general, if a church member approaches you with mental health concerns that we discussed in previous sessions, it is always a good idea to consider a referral to a mental health professional. If you and your client decide to begin your work together, but after a period of time (e.g., 6-8 sessions), your client exhibits more troubling symptoms, or there is no progress toward your goals, then it is time to refer.

Even though you refer someone to a mental health professional, you can continue to provide help in conjunction with that provider. Your client can authorize sharing of information between the two of you in order to coordinate your efforts. Your encouragement and support can enhance the work your client is doing in psychotherapy, which will increase the possibility of a more effective and efficient course of treatment.

## How Do I Refer?

When you are meeting with church members, and you have determined that it would be beneficial or necessary for them to seek professional help, do the following:

- Reflect the concerns that they reveal to you: "It sounds like you are experiencing..."

- Identify how they have dealt with their issues: "So, you have tried..."

- Ask them how their ways of resolving their anxieties, stress, depression, trauma, etc., have worked: "How has... improved, stayed the same or deteriorated as a result of your choices?"

- Invite them to contemplate various options for help: meeting with you, consulting with church pastors or leaders, going to support groups, and beginning treatment with mental health professionals. You might say, "Given what you have indicated, it might be useful to meet with people who are professionally trained to help you in these types of conditions. Would you consider working with...?"

- If you decide to provide a referral, provide information about the referral. It is also important to be positive and encouraging about pursuing help in this way.

- Discuss their reactions to your referral by reflecting their thoughts and feelings.

- Make an informal contract for that person, couple or family to contact the professional as soon as possible.

- Follow-up afterward to ensure that they are getting the help they need.

## To Whom Do I Refer?

There are different types of mental health professionals who can work with individuals, couples, and families suffering from mental disorders. The following is a list of main providers of mental health care:

- A psychologist has a doctoral degree (Ph.D./Psy.D.) whose graduate education consists of academic, research, and clinical experiences, focused on diagnosis, assessment, and treatment of various mental, emotional, relational, and behavioral disorders. In order to be licensed as a psychologist, one has to have at least 3,000 hours of working with patients under supervision, and pass two standardized exams administered by the state licensing board.

- A psychiatrist has a medical degree (M.D.) whose graduate education consists of attending medical school and residency in psychiatry. A psychiatrist's expertise is in medication evaluation, prescription, and treatment. Some can do psychotherapy, but are not trained as extensively as psychologists in this area. Psychiatrists also need to pass their board exams in order to be licensed to practice.

- A marriage and family therapist (MFT) has a master's degree in psychology, counseling, or a related field. MFTs have academic and clinical experiences to treat people with mental disorders. They are required to have 3,000 hours of supervised clinical experience and pass their board exams in order to be licensed in California. The degree and hour requirements may vary depending on the state.

- A licensed clinical social worker (LCSW) has a master's degree in social work and is trained to treat those suffering from mental disorders. In addition, LCSWs can provide case management and advocacy for their clients. Similar to other mental health professionals, in order to be licensed, they need to have certain hours of client contact and pass their board exams.

Your referral may have to take into account one's financial constraints. Depending on their degree, license, experience, and location, these mental health professionals have a wide range of fee structure. Health insurances usually cover treatments for mental disorders. Nonetheless, it is always advisable to check with one's insurance policy for coverage details prior to embarking on any treatments.

*What are some obstacles you can anticipate as you refer your client to a mental health professional?*

---

---

---

More than anything else, it is important to help your church member find a provider who fits well with her needs, values, and personality. For example, for some individuals, gender, age, race, Christian beliefs, and/or marital status might make a difference to how they feel about their counseling experiences. The best predictor of treatment outcome is the relationship between the provider and the client.[1] A relationship where the client feels that his counselor has his best interest at heart, is trustworthy, cares about his issues, and understands him – that is what moves people toward healing and health.

# Session 12

## Legal and Ethical Concerns

As we draw our lay counseling training to a close, we need to address potential legal and ethical issues that may arise as you serve your church as lay counselors. It is essential to be informed about these matters as they can affect how you function in this ministry. Being aware and taking care of these concerns can protect you and the people you are serving from possible negative repercussions from the work you are doing together.

Be advised that each state may have different legal and ethical requirements for lay counselors. I will be referring to California's mandates as I discuss various issues.

### Lay Counseling Ministry Application

After our last session, if you have decided that this ministry is a good fit with your passions and talents, please complete an application to be a lay counselor, and submit this to the leaders who are managing the lay counseling ministry at your church.[1] This application process is a necessary step to ensure that the church has done what it can to increase the likelihood of a positive and healing experience for its members as the latter meet with their lay counselors.

## Supervision

As mentioned at the outset of this training curriculum, supervision, by a mental health professional and/or a pastor who has significant education and experience in counseling, is necessary to have an effective lay counseling ministry. This can take the form of individual or group supervision on a weekly or bi-weekly basis depending on need.

## Informed Consent

When you meet with clients, it is essential to have them understand and agree to the policies and procedures of your lay counseling ministry. Thus, a consent form needs to be read, completed, and signed by your client in the initial meeting.[1] If you are working with a minor, you need to have his parents' consent to work with him. My recommendation is also to review the information with the child client in age-appropriate ways and receive his permission as well. An *Informed Consent* document should contain information about the lay counseling ministry, confidentiality issues, appointment logistics, and emergency plans.

## Confidentiality

As mentioned from the beginning of this ministry, confidentiality is a key component of your service. It is imperative that you keep all information confidential, including whom you are meeting and what was discussed. There are legal exceptions to this confidentiality rule as follows:

- There is a reasonable suspicion of child, dependent, or elder abuse or neglect.

- There is a danger to self, others, or property.

- Your client becomes gravely disabled.

In the event of any of the above situations, please talk with your supervisor immediately to plan and execute legally mandated and ethical measures.

In addition, you may ask for authorization to release information to others involved in your client's life if you determine that this is in the best interest of your client. For example, if your client is working with a psychologist, you might want to ask your client for permission to share information with that professional so that you can work together to provide the greatest help possible. If your client allows you to exchange information with a specific individual(s), then you no longer need to keep the information private from that individual(s).

## Child Abuse

The Child Abuse Reporting Law (California Penal Code section 11166) requires certain people to report any suspected or known abuse and neglect of children to a child protective agency. Child abuse is defined as any intentional physical injury, sexual exploitation and assault, willful cruelty, unlawful corporal punishment, and neglect, of anyone under 18 years old. Please refer to the Department of Social Services site for further information.[2]

## Elder Abuse

Elder is defined as adults age 65 and older, and dependent/disabled adults (ages 18-64) who are unable to live on their own. Elder abuse consists of the following:

- Intentional physical injury, e.g., unreasonable physical restraint and deprivation of food and water

- Sexual assault

- Emotional abuse, e.g., verbal threats and confinement

- Neglect, e.g., not providing adequate medical care

- Financial exploitation, e.g., theft of money or property from an elder

If you suspect or have knowledge of elder abuse, you need to report to an adult protective agency.[3]

## Potential Suicide/Homicide

If your client indicates that she is thinking about harming herself or someone else, it is important to notify appropriate people or agencies to protect people's lives. Again, it is crucial to discuss the situation with your supervisor to decide legal and ethical interventions that are consistent with your state regulations.

## Domestic Violence

If your client is a perpetrator of domestic violence, it is important to assess his potential for harm and set up a plan in anticipation of possible risk to his partner. This may involve increased monitoring of your client, more frequent meetings per week, and consultation with other providers with whom you have permission from your client to share information. If your client is making a specific threat of violence toward his partner, then you have a duty to warn that partner as well as appropriate agencies to protect her life. If this is the case, it is imperative that you discuss the situation with your supervisor and determine the best course of action together.

If you become aware that your client is a victim of domestic violence from her partner, you are not mandated to report. However, it is critical to do all that you can to ensure your client's safety. If the domestic violence involves harm to a child, then you are required to report to the appropriate authorities as mentioned earlier. Again, please consult with your supervisor.

## Boundary Crossings

Boundary issues in lay counseling refer to contact outside the counselor-client session, length of the appointment, location of the meeting, physical touch, and counselor's self-disclosure. Boundary crossings refer to situations that deviate from the normal procedures of counseling. Some of these may be beneficial for your clients, while others may be detrimental to their well-being. For example, meeting at Starbucks or walking with your client rather than meeting in an office may not be standard practice for many counselors. However, these behaviors may be appropriate given certain circumstances. On the other hand, having a sexual relationship of any kind with one's client is absolutely unacceptable. It is highly destructive to one's client and to the counseling relationship. This kind of exploitation of one's client for the counselor's benefit can also occur in other areas, e.g., involving money, and is considered to be unethical, and most likely, illegal.

When you decide to cross certain boundaries, be sure to discuss the situation with your supervisor to ensure that this is in the best interest of the client and enhances the therapeutic value of the work you are doing with your client.


## Writing Notes

One way that you can decrease the likelihood of experiencing legal and ethical problems is by keeping brief records of your meetings together with your clients.[1] Be sure to keep these notes in a locked file or in a secure, encrypted file on your computer, to maintain confidentiality.


## Further Reading

In addition to what was covered in this session, it is mandatory that you read the American Association of Christian Counselors' *Code of Ethics* before you begin your lay counseling ministry.[4] If you have any questions or concerns regarding what you read here or studied during this training, please contact your church leaders and lay counseling ministry supervisors.


## In Conclusion...

I began this curriculum with words from Isaiah 61: 1-3 as this is what I hope we – as God's children and especially as lay counselors – can strive toward:

> *The Spirit of the Sovereign Lord is on me,*
> *because the Lord has anointed me*
> *to proclaim good news to the poor.*
> *He has sent me to bind up the brokenhearted,*
> *to proclaim freedom for the captives and*

*release from darkness for the prisoners,*
*to proclaim the year of the Lord's favor*
*and the day of vengeance of our God,*
*to comfort all who mourn,*
*and provide for those who grieve in Zion —*
*to bestow on them a crown of beauty  instead of ashes,*
*the oil of joy  instead of mourning, and*
*a garment of praise  instead of a spirit of despair.*
*They will be called oaks of righteousness,*
*a planting of the Lord for the display of his splendor. (NIV)*

These are words describing our Lord Jesus Christ, through whom we live and serve. May God bless you and your lay counseling ministry as you seek to follow Jesus' example to facilitate healing and wholeness in the lives of those God brings to you.

# Appendix A

## Lay Counseling Ministry Application

**Name:**_____

**Address:** _____

**Email:**_____

**Phone:** _____

### Personal Information

Please share briefly your faith journey:

_____

_____

_____

What do you believe are your spiritual gifts and talents?

_____

_____

_____

Why do you want to serve in this lay counseling ministry?

_____

_____

_____

## Background Check

Have you ever been convicted of a crime?

☐ Yes ☐ No

If yes, please explain:

_____

_____

Are there any complaints, charges, or investigations pending against you by any licensing or ethics board for misconduct?

☐ Yes ☐ No

If yes, please explain:

_____

_____

Are you aware of any traits/circumstances in which you may pose a threat to others?

☐ Yes ☐ No

If yes, please explain:

_____

_____

## Church Membership

How long have you been a member at this church?

_____

What areas have you served?

_____

**References** (Please provide names and contact information of two individuals who are not related to you)

1. _____

2. _____


## LAY COUNSELOR STATEMENT

I attest and affirm that all the information I have provided in this application is absolutely accurate and true.

I authorize the church and its lay counseling ministry leaders to contact person or entity listed in this application and for that person or entity to provide any information necessary.

I agree to abide by the policies of the church and its lay counseling ministry, and to protect the health and safety of the church members assigned to my care.


Printed Name:_____

Signature:_____

Date: _____

# Appendix B

## Lay Counseling Ministry Informed Consent

This is a church-based ministry providing lay counseling to the members of our church community. We believe that an authentic relationship with God and a biblically consistent life facilitates health. Thus, in our work with you, we will strive to reflect our own faith in God, the model set forth by Jesus Christ in His ministry, and the counsel of the Holy Spirit.

### Confidentiality

All information disclosed is confidential, and may not be revealed to anyone without your permission, except where disclosure is required by law. These exceptions to confidentiality include the following: (a) there is a reasonable suspicion of child, dependent or elder, abuse or neglect; (b) there is a danger to self, others, or property; and/or (c) you become gravely disabled. In addition, our ministry is supervised by a mental health professional, and thus, some information will be shared with our supervisor as needed.

### Appointment Times

Your appointment time has been especially reserved for you. In order to honor your needs and the needs of others, please call at least 24 hours in advance from the time of your appointment if you are unable to make it.

### Emergencies

We are unable to provide emergency care. Thus, in the event of an emergency, please call one of the following numbers: Emergency Psychiatric Services at 408-885-6100, Suicide and Crisis Services at 855-278-4204, or Mental Health Urgent Care at 408-885-7855.

## The Process of Lay Counseling

Participation can result in a number of benefits, including resolution of the specific concerns that led you to seek lay counseling. Working toward these benefits requires your very active involvement, honesty, and openness to change. During your meetings, discussing unpleasant events, feelings, or thoughts can result in your experiencing discomfort (e.g., strong feelings of anger, sadness, and anxiety). There is no guarantee that lay counseling will yield positive or intended results. If you and I find that we are not a "good fit," I will refer you to another lay counselor or to a mental health professional who may be better suited to help you. You are welcome to discontinue counseling at any time.

*I have read and understood all the information on this form. I agree to the above conditions, and consent accordingly to lay counseling.*

Printed Name of Client: _____

Date: _____

Signature of Client: _____

Signature of Parent(s)/Guardian(s): _____

# Appendix C
## Lay Counseling Ministry Registration

Today's Date: _____

Name: _____

Age: _____

Address:_____

Email: _____

Phone: _____

What is the best way to contact and/or leave messages for you?

_____

Marital Status:  ☐ single  ☐ married  ☐ separated  ☐ divorced

Children's names and ages (if any):

_____

_____

If patient is under 18, please give the following information on parent(s) or guardian(s):

Name(s): _____

Address(es): _____

Email Address(es): _____

Phone(s): _____

In the event of an emergency, contact (name & phone number):

_____

What prompted you to seek lay counseling at this time?

_____

_____

_____

Have you had any type of counseling before? If yes, explain:

_____

_____

_____

Are you currently taking any medications? If yes, list the names and the purpose for which you are taking these:

_____

_____

_____

Is there any family history of mental illnesses, alcoholism, and/or violence?

_____

_____

_____

Have you ever attempted suicide? If yes, please explain:

_____

_____

_____

# Appendix D

## Lay Counseling Ministry Meeting Notes

Name: _____

Date: _____

Session Number: _____

Appt. Time: _____

Type of Session:  ☐ Individual  ☐ Couples  ☐ Family  ☐ Group

Who was Present: _____

Concerns Addressed:_____

_____

_____

_____

_____

_____

_____

_____

_____

_____

_____

_____

Next Appointment: _____

Lay Counselor Signature: _____

# References

## Session 1: Model for Lay Counseling in the Church

1. John 8:3-11 (NIV) The teachers of the law and the Pharisees brought in a woman caught in adultery. They made her stand before the group and said to Jesus, "Teacher, this woman was caught in the act of adultery. In the Law Moses commanded us to stone such women. Now what do you say?" They were using this question as a trap, in order to have a basis for accusing him. But Jesus bent down and started to write on the ground with his finger. When they kept on questioning him, he straightened up and said to them, "Let any one of you who is without sin be the first to throw a stone at her." Again he stooped down and wrote on the ground. At this, those who heard began to go away one at a time, the older ones first, until only Jesus was left, with the woman still standing there. Jesus straightened up and asked her, "Woman, where are they? Has no one condemned you?" "No one, sir," she said. "Then neither do I condemn you," Jesus declared. "Go now and leave your life of sin."

2. I Corinthians 12:24-27 (NIV) …But God has put the body together, giving greater honor to the parts that lacked it, so that there should be no division in the body, but that its parts should have equal concern for each other. If one part suffers, every part suffers with it; if one part is honored, every part rejoices with it. Now you are the body of Christ, and each one of you is a part of it.

3. Galatians 6:2, 5 (NIV) Carry each other's burdens, and in this way you will fulfill the law of Christ…each one should carry their own load.

4. I Thessalonians 1:3 (NIV) We remember before our God and Father your work produced by faith, your labor prompted by love, and your endurance inspired by hope in our Lord Jesus Christ.

## Session 2: Building the Relational Context

1.  John 13:13 (NIV) "You call me 'Teacher' and 'Lord,' and rightly so, for that is what I am."

2.  Matthew 20:28 (NIV) "…the Son of Man did not come to be served, but to serve, and to give his life as a ransom for many."

3.  Luke 10:25-37 (NIV) On one occasion an expert in the law stood up to test Jesus. "Teacher," he asked, "what must I do to inherit eternal life?" "What is written in the Law?" he replied. "How do you read it?" He answered, "'Love the Lord your God with all your heart and with all your soul and with all your strength and with all your mind'; and, 'Love your neighbor as yourself.'" "You have answered correctly," Jesus replied. "Do this and you will live." But he wanted to justify himself, so he asked Jesus, "And who is my neighbor?" In reply Jesus said: "A man was going down from Jerusalem to Jericho, when he was attacked by robbers. They stripped him of his clothes, beat him and went away, leaving him half dead. A priest happened to be going down the same road, and when he saw the man, he passed by on the other side. So too, a Levite, when he came to the place and saw him, passed by on the other side. But a Samaritan, as he traveled, came where the man was; and when he saw him, he took pity on him. He went to him and bandaged his wounds, pouring on oil and wine. Then he put the man on his own donkey, brought him to an inn and took care of him. The next day he took out two denarii and gave them to the innkeeper. 'Look after him,' he said, 'and when I return, I will reimburse you for any extra expense you may have.' "Which of these three do you think was a neighbor to the man who fell into the hands of robbers?" The expert in the law replied, "The one who had mercy on him." Jesus told him, "Go and do likewise."

## Session 3: Counseling Tools

1.  Luke 5:16 (NIV) But Jesus often withdrew to lonely places and prayed.

2.  John 11:38-44 (NIV) Jesus, once more deeply moved, came to the tomb. It was a cave with a stone laid across the entrance. "Take away the stone," he said. "But, Lord," said Martha, the sister of the dead man, "by this time there is a bad odor, for he has been there four days." Then Jesus said, "Did I not tell you that if you believe, you will see the glory of God?" So they took away the stone. Then Jesus looked up and said, "Father, I thank you that you have heard me. I knew that you always hear me, but I said this for the benefit of the people standing here, that they may believe that you sent me." When he had said this, Jesus called in a loud voice, "Lazarus, come out!" The dead man came out, his hands and feet wrapped with strips of linen, and a cloth

around his face. Jesus said to them, "Take off the grave clothes and let him go."

3.  Matthew 26:39 (NIV) Going a little farther, he fell with his face to the ground and prayed, "My Father, if it is possible, may this cup be taken from me. Yet not as I will, but as you will."

4.  Benson, H., & Proctor, W. (2010). *Relaxation revolution: Enhancing your personal health through the science and genetics of mind body healing.* New York: Scribner.

5.  Edlmeier, P., Eberth, J., Schwartz, M, Zimmerman, D., Haarig, F. (2012). The psychological effects of meditation: A meta-analysis. *Psychological Bulletin, 138*(6), 1139-1171.

6.  Joshua 1:8 (NIV) Keep this Book of the Law always on your lips; meditate on it day and night, so that you may be careful to do everything written in it. Then you will be prosperous and successful.

7.  Academy for Guided Imagery. (2006). *Guided imagery research articles.* Retrieved from http://www.academyforguidedimagery.com/research/masterbib/index.html

8.  Pennebaker, J. W. (1997). *Opening up: The healing power of expressing emotions.* New York: Guilford Press.

9.  Kanter, J. W., Schildcrout, J. S., & Kohlenberg, R. J. (2005). In vivo processes in cognitive therapy for depression: Frequency and benefits. *Psychotherapy Research, 15*(4), 366–373.

10. Matthew 18: 15-16 (NIV) "If your brother or sister sins, go and point out their fault, just between the two of you. If they listen to you, you have won them over. But if they will not listen, take one or two others along, so that every matter may be established by the testimony of two or three witnesses."

11. Schulenberg, S. E. (2003). Psychotherapy and movies: On using films in clinical practice. *Journal of Contemporary Psychotherapy, 33*(1), 35-48.

## Session 4: Types of Counseling Formats

1.  Luke 18:11 (NIV) The Pharisee stood by himself and prayed: 'God, I thank you that I am not like other people — robbers, evildoers, adulterers — or even like this tax collector.'

2.  Matthew 9:10-12 (NIV) While Jesus was having dinner at Matthew's house, many tax collectors and sinners came and ate with him and his disciples. When the Pharisees saw this, they asked his disciples, "Why does your teacher eat with tax collectors and sinners?" On hearing this, Jesus said, "It is not the healthy who need a doctor, but the sick.

3.  John 4:7 (NIV) When a Samaritan woman came to draw water, Jesus said to her, "Will you give me a drink?"

4.  John 11:1-45 (NIV) Now a man named Lazarus was sick. He was from Bethany, the village of Mary and her sister Martha. (This Mary, whose brother Lazarus now lay sick, was the same one who poured perfume on the Lord and wiped his feet with her hair.) So the sisters sent word to Jesus, "Lord, the one you love is sick." When he heard this, Jesus said, "This sickness will not end in death. No, it is for God's glory so that God's Son may be glorified through it." Now Jesus loved Martha and her sister and Lazarus... "Lord," Martha said to Jesus, "if you had been here, my brother would not have died. But I know that even now God will give you whatever you ask." Jesus said to her, "Your brother will rise again." Martha answered, "I know he will rise again in the resurrection at the last day." Jesus said to her, "I am the resurrection and the life. The one who believes in me will live, even though they die; and whoever lives by believing in me will never die. Do you believe this?" "Yes, Lord," she replied, "I believe that you are the Messiah, the Son of God, who is to come into the world..." When Mary reached the place where Jesus was and saw him, she fell at his feet and said, "Lord, if you had been here, my brother would not have died." When Jesus saw her weeping, and the Jews who had come along with her also weeping, he was deeply moved in spirit and troubled. "Where have you laid him?" he asked. "Come and see, Lord," they replied. Jesus wept. Jesus, once more deeply moved, came to the tomb. It was a cave with a stone laid across the entrance. "Take away the stone," he said... Then Jesus looked up and said, "Father, I thank you that you have heard me. I knew that you always hear me, but I said this for the benefit of the people standing here, that they may believe that you sent me." When he had said this, Jesus called in a loud voice, "Lazarus, come out!" The dead man came out, his hands and feet wrapped with strips of linen, and a cloth around his face. Jesus said to them, "Take off the grave clothes and let him go." Therefore many of the Jews who had come to visit Mary, and had seen what Jesus did, believed in him.

5.  Matthew 14:14-21 (NIV) When Jesus landed and saw a large crowd, he had compassion on them and healed their sick. As evening approached, the disciples came to him and said, "This is a remote place, and it's already getting late. Send the crowds away, so they can go to the villages and buy themselves some food." Jesus replied, "They do not need to go away. You give them something to eat." "We have here only five loaves of bread and two fish," they answered. "Bring them here to me," he said. And he directed the people to sit down on the grass. Taking the five loaves and the two fish and looking up to heaven, he gave thanks and broke the loaves. Then he gave them to the disciples, and the disciples gave them to the people. They all ate and were satisfied, and the disciples picked up twelve basketfuls of

broken pieces that were left over. The number of those who ate was about five thousand men, besides women and children.

6. Cha, S. O., & Cha, Y. B. (2013). *Guest pass: Access to your teen's world.* San Jose: LifeNote Press.

## Session 5: Regarding Mental Health

1. World Health Organization. (2011). *Mental health: A state of well-being.* Retrieved from http://www.who.int/features/factfiles/mental_health/en/

2. Thoits, P. A., Hewitt, L.N. (2001). Volunteer work and well-being. *Journal of Health and Social Behavior, 42*(2), 115-131.

## Session 6: Depressive and Anxiety Disorders

1. Bible.org (2013). *Fear factor (Genesis 15:1-21).* Retrieved from https://bible.org/seriespage/fear-factor-genesis-151-21

2. Isaiah 41:10 (NIV) So do not fear, for I am with you; do not be dismayed, for I am your God. I will strengthen you and help you; I will uphold you with my righteous right hand.

3. American Psychiatric Association (2013). *Diagnostic and statistical manual of mental disorders: DSM-5 (5th ed.).* Washington DC: Author.

4. World Health Organization (2012). *Depression.* Retrieved from http://www.who.int/mediacentre/factsheets/fs369/en/index.html

5. National Institute of Mental Health (2013). *The numbers count: Mental disorders in America.* Retrieved from http://www.nimh.nih.gov/health/publications/the-numbers-count-mental-disorders-in-america/index.shtml#MajorDepressive

6. Centers for Disease Control and Prevention (2013). *CDC finds suicide rates among middle-aged adults increased from 1999-2010.* Retrieved from http://www.cdc.gov/media/releases/2013/p0502-suicide-rates.html

7. National Institute of Mental Health (2013). *The numbers count: Mental disorders in America.* Retrieved from http://www.nimh.nih.gov/health/publications/the-numbers-count-mental-disorders-in-america/index.shtml#Anxiety

## Session 7: Addictions

1.  Yancey, P. (1997). *What's so amazing about grace?* Grand Rapids, Michigan: Zondervan Publishing House.

2.  Substance Abuse and Mental Health Services Administration. (2012). *Results from the 2011 National Survey on Drug Use and Health: Summary of National Findings*, NSDUH Series H-44, HHS Publication No. (SMA) 12-4713. Rockville, MD: Substance Abuse and Mental Health Services Administration.

3.  National Institute on Alcohol Abuse and Alcoholism. (2013). *Alcohol use disorders*. Retrieved from http://www.niaaa.nih.gov/alcohol-health/overview-alcohol-consumption/alcohol-use-disorders

4.  U.S. National Library of Medicine. National Institute of Health. Medline Plus. (2013). *Alcoholism and alcohol abuse*. Retrieved from http://www.nlm.nih.gov/medlineplus/ency/article/000944.htm

5.  Substance Abuse and Mental Health Services Administration. (2012). *Results from the 2011 National Survey on Drug Use and Health: Summary of National Findings*, NSDUH Series H-44, HHS Publication No. (SMA) 12-4713. Rockville, MD: Substance Abuse and Mental Health Services Administration.

6.  Helpguide.org. (2013). *Drug abuse and addiction.* Retrieved from http://www.helpguide.org/mental/drug_substance_abuse_addiction_signs_effects_treatment.htm

7.  Taylor, V. (2013, August 29). Japan to launch 'fasting' camps for Internet-addicted students. *New York Daily News.* Retrieved from http://www.nydailynews.com/life-style/japan-launch-internet-fasting-camps-article-1.1440483

8.  Fackler, M. (2007, November 18). In Korea, boot-camp cure for web obsession. *The New York Times.* Retrieved from http://www.nytimes.com/2007/11/18/technology/18rehab.html?pagewanted=all&_r=0

9.  Weinstein, A., & Lejoyeux, M. (2010). Internet addiction or excessive Internet use. *The American Journal of Drug and Alcohol Abuse, 36*(5), 277-283.

10. Beard, K. W. (2005). Internet addition: a review of current assessment techniques and potential assessment questions. *CyberPsychology & Behavior, 8*(1), 7-14.

## Session 8: Issues of Anger and Violence

1.  Mark 3:5 (NIV) He looked around at them in anger and, deeply distressed at their stubborn hearts...

2.  World Health Organization (2012). *Violence against women.* Retrieved from http://www.who.int/mediacentre/factsheets/fs239/en/

3.  Safe Horizon (2013). *Domestic violence: Statistics and facts.* Retrieved from http://www.safehorizon.org/index/what-we-do-2/domestic-violence--abuse-53/domestic-violence-the-facts-195.html

## Session 9: Childhood Mental Disorders

1.  Mark 10:13-16 (NIV) People were bringing little children to Jesus for him to place his hands on them, but the disciples rebuked them. When Jesus saw this, he was indignant. He said to them, "Let the little children come to me, and do not hinder them, for the kingdom of God belongs to such as these. Truly I tell you, anyone who will not receive the kingdom of God like a little child will never enter it." And he took the children in his arms, placed his hands on them and blessed them.

2.  Centers for Disease Control and Prevention (2013). *Children's mental health – new report.* Retrieved from http://www.cdc.gov/features/childrensmentalhealth/

3.  Kessler, R. C., Chiu, W. T., Demler, O., Merikangas, K. R., Walters, E. E. (2005). Prevalence, severity, and comorbidity of 12-month DSM-IV disorders in the National Comorbidity Survey Replication. *Archives of General Psychiatry, 62*(6). 617-627.

4.  Centers for Disease Control and Prevention (2013). *Children's mental health – new report.* Retrieved from http://www.cdc.gov/features/childrensmentalhealth/

5.  American Psychiatric Association (2013). *Diagnostic and statistical manual of mental disorders: DSM-5 (5ᵗʰ ed.).* Washington DC: Author.

6.  National Institute of Health (2013). *Anxiety disorders.* Retrieved from http://www.nimh.nih.gov/health/topics/anxiety-disorders/index.shtml

7.  National Institute of Health (2013). *Anxiety disorders in children and adolescents.* Retrieved from http://www.nimh.nih.gov/health/publications/anxiety-disorders-in-children-and-adolescents/index.shtml

## Session 10: Personality Disorders

1.  McCrae, R. R., & John, O. P. (1992). An introduction to the five-factor model and its applications. *Journal of Personality, 60*(2), 175-215.

2.   American Psychological Association. (2013). What causes personality disorders. Retrieved from http://www.apa.org/topics/personality/disorders-causes.aspx

3.   American Psychiatric Association (2013). *Diagnostic and statistical manual of mental disorders: DSM-5 (5th ed.)*. Washington DC: Author.

4.   Samuel, D. B. & Widiger, T. A. (2010). A comparison of obsessive-compulsive personality disorder scales. *Journal of Personality Assessment, 92*(3). 232-240.

## Session 11: Self-Evaluation and Referrals

1.   Safran, J.D., Muran, J.C., and Proskurov, B. (2009). Alliance, negotiation, and rupture resolution. In R. L. and S. J. A. (Eds.) *Handbook of Evidence Based Psychodynamic Psychotherapy* (201-205). New York: Humana Press.

## Session 12: Legal and Ethical Concerns

1.   See sample forms in the Appendix section of this curriculum.

2.   Department of Social Services. (2013). *Report abuse*. Retrieved from http://www.cdss.ca.gov/cdssweb/PG20.htm

3.   State of California, Department of Justice. (2013). *Citizen's guide to preventing and reporting elder abuse*. Retrieved from http://oag.ca.gov/bmfea/citizens

4.   American Association of Christian Counselors. (2013). *Code of ethics*. Retrieved from http://www.aacc.net/about-us/code-of-ethics/

# Acknowledgments

Many people have contributed to the process and completion of this book. I am tremendously grateful for the love, support, prayer, and encouragement of all my family and friends.

In addition, thank you, Valerie Plummer, for reading the drafts and giving valuable feedback. I appreciate your generosity in investing time and energy in editing this curriculum. Thank you, Dariel Doyle, for your enthusiastic support and helpful comments on this work. You are a terrific cheerleader. To Carolyn, Maria, Lance, and Kathryn, who deliberated with me on some of the details of this workbook, I am grateful for your input.

I would like to extend my appreciation to my team of lay counselors at OCSJ who trained with this curriculum and are now applying it to their lives. Your thoughtful questions and remarks provided further insight that enriched this book.

Most of all, I thank God for providing me with a vision for lay counseling ministry and being with me throughout this writing process. As with all my work, without God's inspiration, wisdom, and guidance, this training workbook would never have been accomplished.

# About the Author

Susan Oh Cha, Ph.D. is a licensed clinical psychologist. She has worked in various treatment settings: university counseling centers, hospitals, and community mental health agencies. She is committed to facilitating healing and wholeness in individuals, couples, and families through her work in private practice, consultation, writing, speaking, and community service. Dr. Cha also co-wrote *Guest Pass: Access To Your Teen's World* with her daughter, Yumi Cha.

www.ingramcontent.com/pod-product-compliance
Lightning Source LLC
Chambersburg PA
CBHW070804290326
41931CB00011BA/2133